D0161923

The Future Society

Trans-action Books

The Future Society

Edited by
DONALD N. MICHAEL

Trans- **action** Books

Published by
Aldine Publishing Company

The essays in this book originally appeared
in *Trans-* **action** Magazine

Copyright © 1970 by Transaction, Inc.
All Rights Reserved
Printed in the United States of America

TA Book 17
Library of Congress Catalog Number 74-115-946

Contents

Preface

However diverse their attitudes and interpretations may sometimes be, social scientists are now entering a period of shared realization that the United States—both at home and abroad—has entered a crucial period of transition. Indeed, the much burdened word "crisis" has now become a commonplace among black militants, Wall Street lawyers, housewives, and even professional politicians.

For the past seven years, *Trans*-action magazine has dedicated itself to the task of reporting the strains and conflicts within the American system. But the magazine has done more than this. It has pioneered in social programs for changing the society, offered the kind of analysis that has permanently restructured the terms of the "dialogue" between peoples and publics, and offered the sort of prognosis that makes for real alterations in social and political policies directly affecting our lives.

The work done in the pages of *Trans*-action has crossed

professional boundaries. This represents much more than simple cross-disciplinary "team efforts." It embodies rather a recognition that the social world cannot be easily carved into neat academic areas. That, indeed, the study of the experience of blacks in American ghettos, or the manifold uses and abuses of agencies of law enforcement, or the sorts of overseas policies that lead to the celebration of some dictatorships and the condemnation of others, can best be examined from many viewpoints and from the vantage points of many disciplines.

This series of books clearly demonstrates the superiority of starting with real world problems and searching out practical solutions, over the zealous guardianship of professional boundaries. Indeed, it is precisely this approach that has elicited enthusiastic support from leading American social scientists for this new and dynamic series of books.

The demands upon scholarship and scientific judgment are particularly stringent, for no one has been untouched by the current situation. Each essay republished in these volumes bears the imprint of the author's attempt to communicate his own experience of the crisis. Yet, despite the sense of urgency these papers exhibit, the editors feel that many have withstood the test of time, and match in durable interest the best of available social science literature. This collection of *Trans*-action articles, then, attempts to address itself to immediate issues without violating the basic insights derived from the classical literature in the various fields of social science.

The subject matter of these books concern social changes that have aroused the long-standing needs and present-day anxieties of us all. These changes are in organizational life styles, concepts of human ability and intelligence, changing patterns of norms and morals, the relationship of social conditions to physical and biological environments, and in the status of social science with national policy making.

The dissident minorities, massive shifts in norms of social conduct, population explosions and urban expansions, and vast realignments between nations of the world of recent years do not promise to disappear in the seventies. But the social scientists involved as editors and authors of this *Trans*-action series have gone beyond observation of these critical areas, and have entered into the vital and difficult tasks of explanation and interpretation. They have defined issues in a way making solutions possible. They have provided answers as well as asked the right questions. Thus, this series should be conceived as the first collection dedicated not to hightlighting social problems alone, but to establishing guidelines for social solutions based on the social sciences.

THE EDITORS
Trans-action

Introduction

DONALD N. MICHAEL

There is a semantic loading on the word "society" that suggests stability and coherence. This impression is strength-
ened when we use the phrase "the future society"—as if
we are now in one society and, at some vague but somehow
bounded period called the "future," we will live in another.
Recent faddish and serious preoccupation with *the* future,
more specifically with the future of 1976, or 1984, or 2000,
has reinforced this time-boundedness. The pseudo-concrete-
ness of anticipated social structure thus generated is also the
legacy of journalistic standards, author ignorance, and reader receptivity. All encourage attendance to hardware, or
people and institutions treated as hardware, rather than to
the subtleties of human behavior, culture and social process
that, when properly emphasized, make conjecturing about
the future appallingly complicated and open-ended.

These papers taken together make a different contribution to the growing interest in the future society: they

1

destroy the temporal and social boundedness of the usual preoccupations with the future by stressing the *conditions* of *transition* that will characterize at least those years ahead that we can hope to influence by what we do. If the reader will reflect on the implications of each essay for each other essay he will have a better appreciation than he can get from most of the rest of the futurist literature of why the relevant "future society" will not be a stable, coherent state of affairs, clearly differentiated from the present. Instead, these will be times of unrelieved operational, ethical and political turmoil. New knowledge will carry unprecedented potentialities for good or for catastrophic evil. Old institutional and individual standards for "getting ahead" will bedevil us, often dragging us into life-ways that we would not wish to follow. And new institutional and individual ways will confront us with both new opportunities for human growth and new threats to sense of self and survival.

These, then, are essays about "from now on" for as long as it takes to evolve a new social coherence that will be as distinguishable from recent industrial society as was this society from feudal society before it. What "post-industrial," or "post-civilization," or the society of "technological man" might be, will depend on how the only future society we will know—the time of transition—works its way out. For, the circumstances of this working-through will provide still later times with the historical myth and the rationale that will justify the new social forms. Nevertheless, intense attention to this working-through period is what is almost always bypassed in formal futurist essays (though it is central in much sophisticated science fiction).

The remaining paragraphs of this Introduction will not summarize or integrate the following chapters. Instead they are expressions of some of my preoccupations with aspects of the transition as they are related to and stimulated by issues explored in these chapters.

My point of entry has to do with the power-enhancing aspects of social knowledge. We desperately need more knowledge—information related by applicable theory—regarding the nature and conduct of men and institutions if only to be able to keep enough ahead of the pile-up of social needs and demands to sort and respond to them within a feasible allocation of time and human and material resources. The expanding attention to futurism, planning, program budgeting, social indicators, the consequences of technology and so on all demonstrate a growing appreciation of this need. That the present impact and application of such techniques is far less than the imagery about impact and application implies does not vitiate the significance of the fact that organizations and men recognize that they must now at least *look* as if they want to gain and use such knowledge. While bureaucratic resistances and methodological weakness are sufficient to keep the imagery well ahead of the action for as far ahead as we can see, pressures from social engineering advocates as well as those generated by the imagery itself, plus improvements in method and growing social needs will strongly tend to move the action in the direction of the imagery.

Inevitably, then, we will face new questions: Who is to define what knowledge is relevant for a particular application? Who controls access to the sources of information? Who determines how and when information is to be transformed into knowledge about the society—i.e. according to what preferred theory and definitions of social reality? Who legitimizes the policies thereby derived? Who applies them? Finally, who determines what are the effects of a policy in action? This last question is critical since the results of policies in action redefine the "reality" from which the next round of information is drawn, thus beginning again the loop of knowledge and action. There is no equivalent in the human situation to the implacable property of inanimate matter that throws wrong theory back in our experiential teeth. Men create their social reality by the very theories they hold about it, as prophesized in Keniston's chilling chapter and as demonstrated in the commentaries on the *Report From Iron Mountain*.

The oncoming pressures to engineer society and the growing opportunity to obtain the knowledge needed to do so—see Webber and Skedgell herein—suggest a continuing, intense, three-way struggle among (1) those who would use the new knowledge courageously, conscientiously, experimentally and, thereby and above all, openly; (2) those who would use it in conventional ways to attain and maintain power (and this group will increasingly include social technologists themselves); and (3) those who would reject social-technological knowledge as misleading and its application as corrupting. The second and third categories, recognizable as the political pragmatists and the new romantics, seem likely to dominate because they require no change in traditional perspectives or operating styles.

The first category, on the other hand, represents a philosophy of action and an ethic about which we have practically no historical experience that can serve as a basis for organizational arrangements—though there seem to be the beginnings of a mood and fragments of a social structure, as the Bennis and Davis papers can be read to suggest. Various forms of interpersonal explorations such as encounter groups and the commune movement are partial evidence of the rewards and possibilities of such an approach. So too are the few extensive and successful efforts at organizational change involving participant management.

The radical requirement implicit in this approach is that institutions and organizations must operate in a context of values that accepts the naturalness of error and the necessity to embrace error as prerequisite for social learning and hence for social evolution. Widespread acceptance of an error-embracing approach would result in the creation of a learning society, one in which leadership would expect and be expected to believe and to say, openly, "Our (project, program, policy) isn't working the way we thought it would, and this is why. We must try something else now, and this is what. We must evaluate and evaluate, experiment and experiment. We must wait long enough but not put off too long to find out what is happening, to learn whether our knowledge is leading us where we hoped to go. We must remain students of ourselves, of our organizations, and of our environment."

Fundamentally, our organizations are currently designed to disassociate themselves from error, to reject, distort or avoid knowledge by pretending no error occurred or, if it did, that it was somebody else's fault (beginning with the snake in Eden) or that, if nobody can be stuck with it, it really is a trivial error. Especially, our public organizations are designed to bury errors by encouraging relationships between the organization and its relevant environment such that little or no error-indicating feedback is permitted or acknowledged. (A built-in, threat based, error-embracing mechanism of limited value is the profit and loss statement, but even it doesn't work too well as a change stimulator inside large corporations. And outside of management's offices profit and loss is used expediently, hardly candidly, in dealing with the corporation's constituencies such as labor, stockholders, congress, and the communities they are based in.) This is an important reason why organizations much prefer to demonstrate their utility through input measures rather than output measures. And if error-indicating knowledge does manage to filter into the organization, there are endless structural and role arrangements that assure that little if any learning will occur. Usually the rewards of stability take priority over the rewards of change.

We tend to think of the institutions of science and engineering as "error embracing." But as T. Kuhn and J. Conant among others have demonstrated, in science the ideal is infrequently realized. The unnecessary death of three American astronauts and the on-again-off-again revelations that followed were a spectacular but not rare example that the ideal doesn't work well in engineering practice either. What is more, as the organizations in which science and engineering are practiced become larger and more public in their support and constituencies, they become subject to the same organizational pragmatics (also read "politics") as other organizations involved in the public welfare and dependent on public funds. The chief of a large research or development effort never publically acknowledges that it now appears that they've been going in an unproductive direction. This strong disinclination to embrace error openly means scientist and engineering organizations will contribute to, as well as help resolve, conflicts in program or direction that will characterize the transition conditions of the next years.

Add, too, that at no time will our increasing knowledge and improving theory be adequate to the problems we face —including the new problems produced by the consequences of applying inadequate knowledge to social problems. This circumstance will supply another argument to the romantics for rejecting knowledge-based social engineering and policy as intrinsically politically corrupt and ethically misdirected. Thereby, the organizational pragmatists will be doing battle on two fronts: against the political appeal of the romantics on the one hand, and on the other, they will be looking for ways to explain away program failures that inevitably will ensnarl them because their capacity to intervene technologically will be so great while their capacity to anticipate untoward consequences of their interventions will be quite limited. The pressures will be enormous to "cover up" and to retreat to organizational survival tactics by controlling the retrieval and dissemination of information. Yet, in just such situations there is always the possibility that disasters and threats of disasters will open the system to more error-embracing experiments. There is abundant evidence that the threat or fact of disaster often leads to organizational responses to errors previously undetected or ignored. But under such circumstance, deliberative and felicitous changes are unlikely. Men who distrust each other's motives and organizations that give first priority to survival are not likely to stumble into a bright future.

It is in this situation of increasingly potent but delimited knowledge that ethical issues will become more and more vexing for some members of each camp for, as Helen Gouldner's paper demonstrates, the use of the new technologies will increasingly confront us with ethical problems we have never before had to face or formulate. From now on we have the double problem: (1) deriving an ethic appropriate to the imperatives to act in situations of unprecedented complexity, of unprecedented technological potency, and of growing awareness that the unanticipated secondary and tertiary consequences of action may very well overwhelm original intents; and (2) developing means for evolving such an ethic in the presence of traditional moralities which for many years will guide the action of many people. Thus a central issue will be that of constructing an ethical basis for allocating priorities among contending needs and asserted rights in a tumultuous world. What is to be the knowledge base and who will use it to determine who is to have the right to access to it and who is to have the right to impose new technologies? Such questions presage ethical issues that have yet to be faced, much less worked out. And hidden in this general topic is that of the ethics of "invading" privacy to get information about un-anticipated effects in order that there can be more effective social planning—which would include a more responsible and responsive ethic as part of the planning process. Here, certainly, an error-embracing approach will be prerequisite to a felicitous evolution.

From the ways I might close this excursion I choose a personal question, one that I believe is also important to many readers: how to help self and others learn to live in such turmoil and to contribute to the evolution of some-thing more satisfying? To my mind there are no adequate answers to either question: Indeed, I don't believe we know what are most of the useful questions to ask. My present inclination is to emphasize discovering the questions—my-self trying to learn what questions to ask and to help students to learn a questioning mode. The pressures on all of us are great to opt for one or another of the two non-questioning polar positions discussed above but I think neither will do. Asking the right questions requires more than intellectual commitment. Just as with the learning so-ciety, it involves personally embracing error in interper-sonally open ways. And this involves discovering how to trust self and others with one's errors. Very importantly, it involves deliberately seeking to experience situations that produce the errors one must then embrace; i.e., deliberately reorienting one's intellectual and emotional, even physical, self to relevant environments in order to perceive in ways that inspire new questions about those processes that characterize people and social arrangements in transition. It involves taking advocate positions with regard to knowledge and action but in a mood that compels repudiation of one's position or modification of it much sooner and more openly than conventional perspectives and motives usually allow.

I believe one can neither understand much about nor contribute much to the future society just by reading about it. To my mind this volume will be worthwhile if it encourages readers to live in it *now*.

The Politics of Information

MELVIN M. WEBBER

Now that three-fourths of Americans are living in urban places—over 50,000,000 in the vast metropolitan centers of the Boston-New York-Washington strip, Chicago, and Los Angeles alone—more and more information is necessary to handle the immense problems of housing, feeding, healing, educating, transporting, and governing them.

A major push is now under way to improve the quality of information about urban life in America. Throughout the country new information centers (or "data banks") are being established, based upon the large storage capacities of electronic computers. These centers are pooling vast stores of facts about a city's people, its real estate, its traffic, its economy, and its governmental activities. In turn, this wealth of new information is being fed into "simulation models" that mimic the behavior of the city's people, its real estate markets, and its over-all economy. These models are used to pre-test the effects of various public actions, as

11

a guide to government officials in deciding among alternative policies.

There are no doubts about the important roles of these new information centers in guiding policy-making, but there is a widespread belief that the facts they contain are neutral, in that data alone favor no decision over another, no group over another. However, because the decisions and actions that people take are shaped by the kinds of information available to them, the centers are likely to become major agents in the processes of social change.

In a field such as astronomy, one's observations and theoretic generalizations are unlikely to make much difference to the phenomena being observed. The remarkable discoveries in astronomy since the war have led to some striking new theories about the histories of stars and the history of the universe. But the stars and the universe remain wholly unaffected by them. In the social sciences, however, as John Seeley has perceptively described it in *Sociology on Trial,* to report one's observations is to change the phenomenon being observed.

To inform a shopping-center investor about consumer travel behavior and about market potentials is to shape his decisions about shopping-center locations and tenant mix. In turn, those decisions will influence the decisions of merchants, shoppers, house-builders, bankers, and others; and they will thus affect the behavioral and market conditions that were initially observed and reported. To supply the facts about national income distribution, as Leon Keyserling and Michael Harrington recently did, was to set loose a chain of responses that may yet change the facts of distribution that were initially reported. The same sort of thing happens with forecasts, of course, as business-cycle theorists and stock-exchange brokers have long known.

Seemingly straightforward facts about a society's things and events are seldom, if ever, neutral. They inevitably intervene into the workings of the systems they describe. The information supplier—whatever his motives and methods—is therefore inevitably immersed in politics. The kinds of facts he selects to report, the way he presents them, the groups they are distributed to, and the inferences he invites will each work to shape outcomes and subsequent facts.

There is a growing belief that better information will make for better actions. But I find a misconception among some urban planners and social scientists who believe that information, *per se,* is nonpolitical—that, as "pure scientists," they can stand outside the system and, with positivistic detachment, record and explain what they observe. This perception of their functions is patently distorted. The scientist, no less than the politician or the merchant or the family is *inside* the system, and his work affects its workings. He cannot escape the fact that his facts are instruments of change. To play the role of scientist in the urban field is also to play the role of intervener, however indirect and modest the interventions.

This pattern is reinforced by the large amount of political and economic capital that information represents. Information, like money, yields power to those who have it. And, like money, the ways in which it is distributed will determine which groups will be favored and which deprived.

An urban intelligence center, quite like the spy or the tipster, cannot be a neutral informant. Even if somehow it succeeded in becoming a nonpartisan supplier of information—making its findings available to all comers—this, too, would represent a powerful intervention into economic, political, and social processes. To redistribute information in such fashion would dramatically change the rules of the

political and economic games that are played in the metropolitan areas where vital information is not fully available
to all. To reduce secrecy would reduce the advantages that
now redound to those favored few who are in on the
secrets. To reduce ignorance among those groups that cannot now afford the high costs of good intelligence would
strengthen their political and economic positions.

Of course, nothing even approximating equality of access
to information is likely, even if an information center were
to be established and supported by a diversified group of
governments, industries, and foundations. The power that
such a center would represent is already clear to many.
Indeed, this is one of the reasons that supporting funds
have been hard to get. But as such centers are established,
we can expect a growing partisan competition to gain
control over their activities and to limit outputs; for some
sorts of information can be very dangerous weapons.

Thus, the social scientists who staff them will immediately find themselves intimately involved in the internal
politics over the centers' programs, mirroring the external
politics of the metropolis. Which studies should be conducted? Which hypotheses favored? Which models em-
ployed? Which data collected? Which variables accounted?
Which analyses made? Which forecasts attempted? Which
alternatives explored? Which conclusions reported? And
which findings and recommendations reported to which of
the competing groups? The staff may wish to believe that
their answers are merely scientific conclusions. Simultaneously, however, they would also be political answers of a
straightforward sort.

Each group in an urban area seeks its own survival, its
own special advantages, its own unique perceptions of self
interest and public welfare. Thus, an elected official may
promote a costly public-works project as a way of stabiliz-

ing his political position. If the analyst should fail to include those so-called "noneconomic variables" in calculating expected returns from the investment, he misses the main point. If he does account for them, he aligns himself with the interests of one partisan group against others. Similarly, a businessmen's group may seek to redevelop a section of the central business district, ostensibly to "revitalize the city's heart" and thereby to "serve the public interest." Unless the analyst is alert to the real business motives driving the project, his information may not give them the indicators of success they really want. If, on the other hand, he *should* serve their purposes, he aligns himself with the project's proponents and against the opponents.

I use these rather homey examples to say that the man who pursues the urban information sciences also chooses a career in politics, for he cannot avoid becoming a protagonist. He becomes a policy-shaper, if not a policy-maker. For, in addition to being a producer of new facts, an identifier and evaluator of potential action-courses, and a prophet of the future, he also plays the role of planner. By supplying information and reporting scientific findings, he thereby says not only what might happen, but what he thinks ought to happen.

His advice must be even more direct than that, however. The socially responsible student, or planner, or scientist—choose whichever name you happen to like best—has an inherent and an ethical obligation to say what he *thinks* ought to be, just as the physician is obligated to advise his patient to submit to unpleasant therapy or the Federal Reserve System's economist to urge adjustment in the rediscount rate.

The ablest students of human problems have often known their clients' wants better than the clients have, and they often know better what the clients should do. With their superior knowledge of the system's structure, its processes, and the wants of the various publics, the planners who can draw upon an elaborate information center would be well-equipped to design action-programs having high odds of bringing high welfare returns.

In this respect, the scientist-politician-planner may be a peculiar breed in the political scene. He is surely a member of a professional interest group composed of peers who share his particular frames-of-reference and, hence, his social objectives. With them, he sees the world through special filters and holds vested interests in certain concepts, analytic methods, and social programs. With them, he tries to sell his particular brands of rationality and his particular images of the social welfare. In these respects he resembles the members of political parties, trade associations, and civic clubs.

But his special character mirrors the special character of science. To a degree far less common in other interest groups, he has learned to *doubt*. He has been trained to question his beliefs, his data, and his findings; to submit his conclusions to critical evaluation by his peers; to tolerate uncertainty and ambiguity; to bear the frustrations of not knowing, and of knowing he does not know; and, by far the most important, to adopt the empirical test for validity.

Along with improved facts, improved modes of predicting, and the disciplined imagination that the new scientific talent is bringing, it is also injecting the scientific morality into urban policy-making. Partisanship, parochialism, and partial knowledge are inherent to the urban system, as they are to science. The intelligence centers can never eliminate them. The new planners must accept them as facts, no less real and valid than rents, transport costs, interest rates, and topographic conditions. But by more systematically accounting for these variables, and by then exposing alternative action and value hypotheses to critical and systematic examination, those in the information-and-planning sciences may help to eliminate the most negative consequences of partisanship and of ignorance. By offering up their own preferred images of private and public welfare, their own perceptions of good ends and means, and their own proposals for social programs, the new species of scientifically trained urban planners are likely to make significant contributions to relieving the more severe social problems that now mark our cities.

November/December 1965

How Computers Pick
an Election Winner

ROBERT A. SKEDGELL

When the American electorate goes to the polls in November many winners of statewide races will be announced on radio and television long before any substantial portion of the tabulated or popular vote is available. Also, many important reasons for their victories will be clear at early stages in the vote counting.

This "clairvoyance" will spring from an extensive use of computerized vote projections, based on quickly reported returns from a small number of selected precincts throughout the country. The radio and television networks will put more trust in, and be more dependent upon, their computers than at any time since they sniffed the first 1960 returns—and proclaimed that the odds were 100 to one that Richard M. Nixon would be the next President of the United States.

One system of computer projections—Vote Profile Analysis used by CBS News—has recorded an average deviation of less than 1 percent in estimating the winners' final percentages in 135 elections. It was developed *after* the 1960 general elections by CBS News, Louis Harris & Associates, and the International Business Machines Corporation. VPA was the first effective and accurate system of drawing scientific samples of the electorate so that a small number of key returns would produce close estimations of election outcomes.

Earlier computer systems were excessively rigid because proper weighting was not given to the individual factors involved. So the first scattered returns from just one or two states tended to unduly influence the vote estimates for the entire nation. The resulting projections for major candidates were inflated—more imputed than computed.

The networks did not suffer great embarrassment over the initial performances of their computerized reporting. They had stashed the machines away practically out of sight of the TV cameras and were prepared to drop them entirely at the first suspicious prognostication; in that event, the computers were to be mere comedy gimmicks, more to be belittled than pitied. If, on the other hand, reasonable forecasts seemed to be forthcoming, the broadcasters could claim credit for fathering a rousing advance in the art of election reporting.

Vote Profile Analysis was unveiled in the off-year elections of 1962. The system was applied to 13 key contests in eight states, and it produced accurate results in twelve—up to two hours ahead of the other networks. In the thirteenth race covered that night, the Massachusetts' gubernatorial contest between John Volpe and Endicott Peabody, VPA indicated the outcome as "too close to call." More than a month went by before Peabody was officially designated the winner by a tiny margin of the more than 2,000,000 votes cast.

One other VPA projection that same night pointed up the power and value of the new election reporting tool. At 10:05 p.m., Eastern time, CBS News reported—on the basis of VPA—that George Romney was the evident winner over John Swainson. The tabulated vote at that moment read:

SWAINSON 310,000
ROMNEY 236,000

Both Romney and Swainson were as disbelieving as the viewers.

What had happened was that VPA had correctly established that Swainson was running behind his necessary (and expected) strength in Wayne County, and that his showing in the Detroit suburbs was down from two years earlier when he won the governorship. When the computer digested these facts and performed the necessary arithmetic, the projected estimate for Romney came out to 52 percent of the vote. His final, official figure was 51.4 percent.

A modified form of VPA was utilized in the 1964 presidential year in the CBS News coverage of important primary races. From New Hampshire to California, VPA demonstrated its preciseness in pointing to the winners early and accurately. The VPA estimate for Henry Cabot Lodge in the New Hampshire contest was precisely the 35.3 percent of the vote which he officially received; in Oregon, VPA projected that Nelson Rockefeller would win 32.9 percent of the vote, and he won exactly that much.

On November 3, 1964, VPA was put to its first full test—it was applied to a total of 107 contests, including the presidential race in 48 states (excluding Alaska and Hawaii) and the District of Columbia. The average deviation between the final VPA estimates in those 107 races and the final, official returns was less than one percent.

There is no witchcraft about VPA. For all its seeming omniscience, it is simply a formalized effort at systematizing voting data. Its essential function is to measure movement of a particular electorate from their voting history, and to present those findings in an orderly manner. Although it is a sophisticated sampling instrument, it is capable of erring, and proper guidelines must be erected to hold mistakes within acceptable limits.

It is an exercise in simple arithmetic—if there were no rush for the results, it could be done by hand. The computer's contribution to the process—and its only contribution—is to store past voting information for the political units selected; to compare the new results from the special precincts with the old; and to extrapolate an estimate of the final result any time such a projection is requested. Once this point in the process is reached, mortal man takes over to analyze the machine's computations and make judgments based upon political, not arithmetical, knowledge.

The cornerstone of Vote Profile Analysis is the model of the electorate to be measured in any election. The model is a kind of portrait in miniature of all the voters of a political unit. It has been likened to screening out most of the dots which comprise a newspaper photograph; if a careful selection were made of the dots to remain, the picture would still be recognizable.

As electorates differ from each other, so do models differ. There is no magic formula which will produce a universal model. Each is custom built. For example, the model for the Republican electorate voting in the California primary this year was 90 precincts, selected to represent in their proper proportions the more than 30,000 precincts in the state. In 1964, the model for the Oregon electorate was 42 precincts which served as a microcosm of that state's 3,255 precincts.

The number of precincts in a model is set on the basis of having few enough to process quickly on election night, but still enough to represent the state's voters faithfully.

Louis Harris knew from his wide experience in politics and polling that people tend to vote in patterns by groups; the patterns are discernible through the extensive research conducted on voting behavior, and through past polling. The assumption that voters of similar background display similar voting behavior is not to say that all members of a group will vote the same. It simply says that if the rural voters in a state vote 72 percent Democratic, 72 out of every 100 ruralites are performing one way, and 28 out of every 100 are performing another way. Nevertheless, the 72 to 28 ratio is an identifiable pattern which will hold true for all of the rural dwellers in the state.

Every political unit in the nation is made up of groups of voters whose voting patterns can be similarly determined. Harris reasoned that:
—if a small sample could be drawn to represent all of the important groups comprising an electorate by their proportionate voting strengths,
—and if a method could be devised to keep track of their votes on election night,
—and to compare those results with the past voting performance of the same groups,
—then it would be possible to project an accurate result.

To begin with, it would be necessary to determine for each state just what the components of the electorate were, what their history of voting has been, and what proportion of the total vote each group would contribute. In order to accomplish this initial process, teams of researchers pored through Bureau of Census records, demographic reports, and other statistical data. Because there is no central record of precinct results for all states, the researchers had to visit many of the county courthouses around the country and dig out the returns from beneath piles of dust. They studied boundary maps of the precincts to determine if changes had occurred since the last election, for in comparing new returns with the old, it is vital that the perimeters of the current precinct match exactly those of the same precinct as it existed before.

With the initial phase of the research completed, the Louis Harris organization drew up a "recipe" for a model —a specification designed to direct the researchers to the to the kinds of precincts which would ultimately fit the model. If the research indicated that 10 of the model precincts would be metropolitan units, the recipe pointed to the *types* of metropolitan precincts which would qualify as representative of their group.

Each of the precincts in the state models designed for the 1964 elections—nearly 2,000 of them—was classified in four ways:

—by geographic section of the state;
—by the size of community;
—by the ethnic background of a vast majority of the residents;
—and by their religious background.

In Harris' view, each of these four dimensions was a "cutting edge" in the politics of 1964 which would serve to measure political behavior. Economic and social classifications were not used as bases for the VPA controls because of the great difficulty in establishing standards which would apply with equal precision in all sections of the nation. A weekly income of $200 in New York City would produce a standard of living and a political outlook quite different from the same weekly income in a small city elsewhere. The economic status of the model precincts was utilized as an informational guide only and not as a component of the extrapolation formula.

To make certain that the precincts gathered under the terms of the recipe fully qualified for the model, researchers spent many months traveling through and around them. They talked to county and precinct officials and to pastors and rabbis to verify the ethnic and religious background of the residents. They read doorbell names as an additional check.

When the researchers returned from the field, they brought with them data on hundreds of precincts which would meet the technical requirements of the recipe, making them eligible to be among the chosen few to comprise the model. The question then remained: of the hundreds of qualified precincts, which combination of 32 or 40 or 50 would best represent all the voters of the state? For example, of all the precincts classified as predominantly White Anglo-Saxon Protestant, which among them would best portray the political behavior of all of the WASP precincts around the state? Put another way, which combination of precincts meeting all of the weighting criteria of the model would come closest to reproducing or reconstructing the past statewide vote for a particular candidate?

To help find the solution, the computer was put to work running off combination after combination of precincts, averaging their past vote, and comparing them to the statewide average, not for just one past election, but several. The best combinations reproduced past results with only one-tenth or two-tenths of one percent deviation. This process of combining precincts continued section by section until the best grouping for an entire state emerged.

As illustration, VPA for Missouri in the 1964 general elections consisted of 40 precincts assembled to accurately represent more than 4,400 precincts. Missouri was divided into five sections: the St. Louis area and the Kansas City area, the great urban anchor points of the whole state; the rural north, which included St. Joseph; the Ozark country in the southeast; and, the southwest including Springfield. In effect, the geographical map of the state was converted to a political map, with the sectional boundaries marking different kinds of voting behavior.

Since research showed that 33 percent of the electorate resided in the St. Louis area, 33 percent of the model precincts (13 of 40) must be located in that area. Kansas City held 20 percent of the vote (8 of 40 precincts). The remaining three sections of the state produced the other 19 precincts of the model.

This procedure was followed for the other VPA categories: size of place, ethnic composition, and religion. The profile for Missouri showed that 28 percent of the electorate resided in large cities; so 12 of the 40 precincts would come from the large cities. Negro voters would comprise about 8 percent of the vote; so 3 precincts were predominantly Negro.

When the final returns from the Missouri VPA precincts were reported to CBS News election headquarters, and the computer compared those results with the past history of those same precincts, it calculated that Lyndon Johnson would carry the state with a percentage of 63.9. The final, official figure for him was 64.0 percent.

It is seldom necessary to wait for all of the precincts in a particular model to report before the analysts make their decision. More often, those "calls" are made on the basis of partially filled models, when, perhaps, half or fewer of the precincts have reported. It is precisely at this point that the men take over from the machines, bringing their political intelligence to bear on the computer's calculations.

In the Missouri election, only 10 of the 40 model precincts had reported at the time that CBS News posted Johnson as the winner.

Because of the four-way classification of Missouri's voters, and because the computer makes a rapid comparison of the new vote with the old, it was easy for the political analysts to determine that the President was running well ahead of Senator Goldwater in each of the five sections of the state, and was getting strong support from all of the major groups of voters. Armed with that kind of detailed information which, of course, the running popular vote total could not provide for hours, the analysts at the CBS News decision desk felt no qualms about picking a winner.

There are times, however, when partial model interpretations can be dangerous, as CBS News, Louis Harris, and IBM discovered last year in the New York City Democratic primary contest. One of the races pitted Oren Lehman against Mario Procaccino for nomination as city controller. When 20 of the 50 VPA precincts had reported their results, there were definite and strong trends for Lehman. Accordingly, the decision was made to post Lehman as the "indicated winner." A little later, as more of the special VPA results came in, the Lehman trend was less strong, and another decision was made to move Lehman from the "indicated" winner's circle to "probable" winner. Still later, when the entire model was complete, the computers calculations suggested to the analysts that the race was, in fact, "too close to call," and Lehman was hence shifted downward another notch. Several hours later, the tabulated vote showed that Procaccino was first catching up, then taking over the lead, and finally was the victor by a slight margin. Procaccino came to the CBS studios to be interviewed in the early morning hours and won the eternal gratitude of all assembled when he refrained from rubbing salt into VPA's wound.

It developed that the city's Jewish Democrats had split their vote sharply in the controller's race, with the Manhattan Jews going strongly for Lehman, and the Bronx and Brooklyn Jews, with a more conservative political tradition, throwing their support to Procaccino, who was running on the so-called "regular party" ticket. When the initial decision was made to name Lehman the "indicated" winner, the special VPA returns from the Manhattan election districts had reported, and they were mistakenly taken as setting the pattern to be expected for all Jewish voters. The subsequent reports from Brooklyn and the Bronx reversed the Lehman trend. Had they been received before or at the same time as the returns from the Manhattan Jewish precincts, the closeness of the race would have been apparent.

Now that computerized vote projections work satisfactorily, the cry is still raised that reporting systems such as VPA take all the fun out of the good old American tradition of waiting for the returns. But it was only a very short time ago that there was considerable, not to say painful, misunderstanding of vote projection. This lack of understanding was fanned inadvertently by the creators of the systems, who found it difficult under the time and competitive pressures of election broadcasting to introduce explanations of the projections with the same impact and prominence as the results. Nowhere was this fact demonstrated more dramatically than in the California Republican primary on June 2, 1964, which squared off Barry Goldwater against Nelson Rockefeller.

At 7:22 p.m., Pacific time, just 22 minutes after some but not all of the polls had closed throughout the state, CBS News reported on the basis of VPA that Goldwater was the winner. What developed through the remainder of that evening, and into the early morning hours of June 3, was enough to try the souls of the CBS News executives who carried the responsibility for the decision.

That decision for Goldwater was based principally on the fact that the first special VPA returns showed him to be making a very strong run in areas where a considerable portion of the Republican electorate resided, especially in Los Angeles County. When the early VPA results were examined by the analysts, it was evident to them that no matter how the vote went in the sections still polling, Rockefeller just could not catch up.

But almost everyone else, on the basis of early returns, thought Rockefeller would win. The trouble was, the tabulated vote as collected and reported by the Associated Press and United Press International did not reflect Goldwater's strong performance in Los Angeles and in Orange and San Diego counties until many hours after the early evening announcement by CBS that Goldwater had won. In fact, the count by the press services at six o'clock the next morning still did not reflect Goldwater's true strength in the southern counties, and Rockefeller seemed to be holding a slim edge. This incomplete wire service tally gave rise to many confusing reports; one San Francisco paper headlined in its afternoon edition the next day, TV PRATFALL—FAST COUNT. ROCKY SWEEPS INTO LEAD. Appearances notwithstanding, the New York governor had not led at any time.

VPA's critics, both professional and lay, have held that it is a divisive force on the body politic; that to report elections in terms of how the various ethnic and religious groups perform is an unhealthy, not to say un-American, approach. Irate viewers called the CBS studios following the New York City elections last year to complain about the undue emphasis they thought had been placed upon what Jewish voters had done, or the Italian-Americans, or the

Irish-Americans. It was demonstrable, however, that these groups did behave in voting patterns—they were the "cutting edge" in deciding between two major tickets which were neatly balanced with one Jew each, one Irish-American each, one Italian-American, and one white Anglo-Saxon Protestant.

Another widespread charge leveled at computerized voting projections is that they influence voters in those sections of the country where polls remain open longer; that citizens in the Western states either change their vote to join the so-called bandwagon as reported from the East Coast, or simply decide not to vote at all. Three social scientists, Harold Mendelsohn of the University of Denver and Kurt Lang and Gladys Engel Lang of the State University of New York at Stony Brook, studied a sample of California voters following the 1964 elections to assess the validity of such charges. Their independent investigations could find no basis for the assertions that anyone changed his intention to vote for Johnson because the network broadcasts reported that he was the apparent winner, nor that anyone planning to vote for Goldwater refrained from doing so because it was forecast that he would lose badly.

Mendelsohn had interviewed a voter sample on the night before the election to ascertain their preferences. After the polls closed, he interviewed the same persons to see if anyone had changed his mind. The result was that no matter whether the voters had tuned in election broadcasts, 96 to 97 percent voted as they intended. Not more than 2 percent of those interviewed switched their vote, and those last-minute changes that did occur followed no discernible pattern.

VPA and the other vote projection systems were born of the need to fill the information vacuum existing between the time the polls close and the tabulation of sufficient votes to indicate an election trend. Had VPA been operating in the 1960 presidential race, the public would have known that at the time Kennedy seemed to be piling up a commanding lead, the final result would actually be extremely close.

In many states the vote counting process remains excruciatingly slow. Some precinct officials are content to interrupt the tabulation for dinner, a good night's sleep, and a leisurely completion and reporting of the count on the following morning, just as they have done for years. There have been proposals advanced to bring the states' election laws into some orderly scheme. Some have called for a uniform period of voting across the country; others have asked for a common poll closing time; still others have advocated a much more widespread use of electronic and mechanical ballot counters which have been introduced in places with varying degrees of success.

One day the states' antiquated election machinery will be brought into the twentieth century; but it will not occur this year, nor probably for some time to come. In the meantime, reporters will continue to utilize every means available to them to bring the election stories to the public as quickly and accurately as possible.

November 1966

Post Bureaucratic Leadership

WARREN G. BENNIS

In an early issue of this magazine (*Trans*-action, June-July 1965), I forecast that in the next 25 to 50 years we would participate in the end of bureaucracy as we know it and in the rise of new social systems better suited to the 20th century demands of industrialization. The prediction was based on the evolutionary principle that every age develops an organizational form appropriate to its genius, and that the prevailing form today—the pyramidal, centralized, functionally specialized, impersonal mechanism known as *bureaucracy*—was out of joint with contemporary realities.

This breakdown of a venerable form of organization so appropriate to 19th century conditions is caused, I argued, by a number of factors, but chiefly the following four: 1) rapid and unexpected change; 2) growth in size beyond what is necessary for the work being done (for example, inflation caused by bureaucratic overhead and tight

33

controls, impersonality caused by sprawls, outmoded rules, and organizational rigidities) ; 3) complexity of modern technology, in which integration between activities and persons of very diverse, highly specialized competence is required; 4) a change in managerial values toward more humanistic democratic practices.

Organizations of the future, I predicted, will have some unique characteristics. They will be adaptive, rapidly changing *temporary systems,* organized around problems-to-be-solved by groups of relative strangers with diverse professional skills. The groups will be arranged on organic rather than mechanical models; they will evolve in response to problems rather than to programmed expectations. People will be evaluated, not in a rigid vertical hierarchy according to rank and status, but flexibly, according to competence. Organizational charts will consist of project groups rather than stratified functional groups, as is now the case. Adaptive, problem-solving, temporary systems of diverse specialists, linked together by coordinating executives in an organic flux—this is the organizational form that will gradually replace bureaucracy.

Ironically, the bold future I had predicted is now routine and can be observed wherever the most interesting and advanced practices exist. Most of these trends are visible and have been surfacing for years in the aerospace, construction, drug, and consulting industries as well as professional and research and development organizations, which only shows that the distant future now has a way of arriving before the forecast is fully comprehended.

A question left unanswered, however, has to do with leadership. How would these new organizations be managed? Are there any transferable lessons from present managerial practices? Do the behavioral sciences provide any suggestions? How can these complex, ever-changing, free-form, kaleidoscopic patterns be coordinated? Of course there can be no definitive answers, but unless we can understand the leadership requirements for organizations of the future, we shall inevitably back blindly into it rather than cope with it effectively.

Accepted theory and conventional wisdom concerning leadership have a lot in common. Both seem to be saying that the success of a leader depends on the leader, the led, and the unique situation. This formulation—abstract and majestically useless—is the best that can be gleaned from over 100 years of research on "leadership."

On the other hand, any formulations may be inadequate and pallid compared to the myths and primitive psychological responses that surround such complexities as leadership and power. Our preoccupation with the mystiques of the Kennedys is sufficient reminder of that.

Thus, leadership theory coexists with a powerful and parallel archetypal reality. But in what follows, we shall see that it is the latter myth that is threatened—the aggressive, inner-directed 19th century autocrat. For the moment, though, I want to quickly review some of the key situational features likely to confront the leader of the future.

The overarching feature is change itself, its accelerating rate and its power to transform. The phrase "the only constant is change" has reached the point of a cliché, which at once anesthetizes us to its pain and stimulates grotesque fantasies about a Brave New World with no place in the sun for us. Change is the "godhead" term for our age as it has not been for any other. One has only to recall that the British Parliament was debating in the last part of the 19th century whether to close up the Royal

Patent Office, as it was felt that all significant inventions had already been discovered.

But what are the most salient changes affecting human organization, the ones with most relevance to their governance? Foremost is the changing nature of our institutions. In 1947, employment stood at approximately 58 million and now is at about 72 million. According to V. K. Fuchs, "Virtually all of this increase occurred in industries that provide services, for example, banks, hospitals, retail stores, and schools." This nation has become the only country to employ more people in services than in production of tangible goods. The growth industries today, if we can call them that, are education, health, welfare, and other professional institutions. The problem facing organizations is no longer manufacturing—it is the management of large-scale sociotechnical systems and the strategic deployment of high-grade professional talent.

There are other important correlates and consequences of change. For example, the working population will be younger, smarter, and more mobile. Half of our country's population is under 25, and one out of every three persons is 15 years of age or younger. More people are going to college; over half go to college in certain urban areas. The United States Postal Department reports that one out of every five families changes its address every year.

Most of these changes compel us to look beyond bureaucracy for newer models of organizations that have the capability to cope with contemporary conditions. The general direction of these changes—toward more service and professional organizations, toward more educated, younger, and mobile employees, toward more diverse, complex, science-based systems, toward a more turbulent and uncertain environment—forces us to consider new styles of leadership. Leading the enterprise of the future becomes a significant social process, requiring as much, if not more, managerial than substantive competence. Robert McNamara is a case in point. Before he came to Washington, he was considered for three Cabinet positions: Defense, State, and Treasury. His "only" recommendation was that he was a superior administrator. Chris Argyris has concluded that success or failure in the United States Department of State depends as much or more on one's interpersonal and managerial competence as one's substantive knowledge of "diplomacy." It can also be said that leadership of modern organizations depends on new forms of knowledge and skills not necessarily related to the primary task of the organization. In short, the pivotal function in the leader's role has changed away from a sole concern with the substantive to an emphasis on the interpersonal and organizational processes.

One convenient focus for a discussion of leadership is to review the main problems confronting modern organizations, and to understand the kinds of tasks and strategies linked to the solution of these problems.

Contributions and Inducements

A simple way to understand this problem is to compute the ratio between what an individual gives and what he gets in his day-to-day transactions. In other words, are the contributions to the organization about equivalent to the inducements received? Where there is a high ratio between inducements and contributions, either the organization or the employee gets restless and searches for different environments, or different people.

There is nothing startling or new about this formulation. Nevertheless, organizations frequently do not know what is truly rewarding, especially for the professionals and highly trained workers who will dominate the organizations of the future. With this class of employee, conventional policies and practices regarding incentives, never particularly sensitive, tend to be inapplicable.

Most organizations regard economic rewards as the primary incentive to peak performance. These are not unimportant to the professional, but, if economic rewards are equitable, other incentives become far more potent. Avarice, to paraphrase Hume, is *not* the spirit of industry, particularly of professionals. Professionals tend to seek such rewards as full utilization of their talent and training; professional status (not necessarily within the organization, but externally with respect to their profession) ; and opportunities for development and further learning. The main difference between the professional and the more conventional, hourly employee is that the former will not yield "career authority" to the organization.

The most important incentive, then, is to "make it" professionally, to be respected by professional colleagues. Loyalty to an organization may increase if it encourages professional growth. (I was told recently that a firm decided to build all future plants in university towns in order to attract and hold on to college-trained specialists.) The "good place to work" resembles a super-graduate school, alive with dialogue and senior colleagues, where the employee will not only work to satisfy organizational demands, but, perhaps primarily, those of his profession.

The other incentive is self-realization, personal growth that may not be task-related. I'm well aware that that remark questions four centuries of an encrusted Protestant ethic, reinforced by the indispensability of work for the preservation and justification of existence. But work, as we all must experience it, serves at least two psychic functions: first, that of binding man more closely to reality; and secondly, in Freud's terms, "of displacing a large amount of libidinal components, whether narcissistic, aggressive, or even erotic, onto professional work and onto human relations connected with it . . ."

It is not at all clear as to how, or even if, these latter needs can be deliberately controlled by the leadership. Company-sponsored courses, sensitivity training sessions, and other so-called adult education courses may, in fact, reflect these needs. Certainly attitudes toward "continuing education" are changing. The idea that education has a terminal point and that college students come in only 4 sizes—18, 19, 20, and 21—is old-fashioned. A "dropout" should be redefined to mean anyone who hasn't *returned* to school.

Whichever way the problem of professional and personal growth is resolved, it is clear that many of the older forms of incentives, based on the more elementary needs (safety-economic-physiological) will have to be reconstituted. Even more profound will be the blurring of the boundaries between work and play, between the necessity to belong and the necessity to achieve, which 19th century mores have unsuccessfully attempted to compartmentalize.

The Problem of Distributing Power

There are many issues involved in the distribution of power: psychological, practical, and moral. I will consider only the practical side, with obvious implications for the other two. To begin with, it is quaint to think that one man, no matter how omniscient and omnipotent, can comprehend, let alone control, the diversity and complexity of the modern organization. Followers and leaders who think this is possible get trapped in a child's fantasy of absolute power and absolute dependence.

Today it is hard to realize that during the Civil War, "government" (Lincoln's executive staff) had fewer than 50 civilian subordinates, and not many executives at that, chiefly telegraph clerks and secretaries. Even so recent an administration as Franklin Roosevelt's had a cozy, "family" tone about it. According to his doctor, for example, Roosevelt "loved to know everything that was going on and delighted to have a finger in every pie."

"Having a finger in every pie" may well be an occupational disease of presidents, but it is fast becoming outmoded. Today's administration must reflect the necessities imposed by size and complexity. In fact, there has been a general tendency to move tacitly away from a "presidential" form of power to a "cabinet" or team concept, with some exceptions (like Union Carbide) where "team management" has been conceptualized and made explicit. There is still a long-standing pseudomasculine tendency to disparage such plural executive arrangements, but they are on the increase.

This system of an "executive constellation" by no means implies an abdication of responsibility by the chief executive. It should reflect a coordinated effort based on the distinct competencies of the individual. It is a way of multiplying executive power through a realistic allocation of effort. Of course, this means also that top executive personnel are chosen not only on the basis of their unique talents but on how these skills and competencies fit and work together.

Despite all the problems inherent in the executive constellation concept—how to build an effective team, compatibility, etc.—it is hard to see other valid ways to handle the sheer size and overload of the leader's role.

The Control of Conflict

Related to the problem of developing an effective executive constellation is another key task of the leader—building a climate in which collaboration, not conflict, will flourish. An effective, collaborative climate is easier to experience and harder to achieve than a formal description of it, but most students of group behavior would agree that it should include the following ingredients: flexible and adaptive structure, utilization of individual talents, clear and agreed-upon goals, standards of openness, trust, and cooperation, interdependence, high intrinsic rewards, and transactional controls—which means a lot of individual autonomy, and a lot of participation making key decisions.

Developing this group "synergy" is difficult, and most organizations take the easy way out—a "zero-synergy" strategy. This means that the organization operates under the illusion that they can hire the best individuals in the world, and then adopt a Voltairean stance of allowing each to cultivate his own garden. This strategy of isolation can best be observed in universities, where it operates with great sophistication. The Berkeley riots were symptomatic of at least four self-contained, uncommunicating social systems (students, faculty, administration, regents) without the trust, empathy and interaction—to say nothing of the tradition—to develop meaningful collaboration. To make matters worse, academics by nature, reinforced by tradition, see themselves as "loners." They want to be independent together, so to speak. Academic narcissism goes a long way on the lecture platform, but may be positively dysfunctional for developing a community.

Another equally pernicious strategy with the same effects, but different style (and more typical of American business institutions), is a pseudodemocratic "groupiness" characterized by false harmony and avoidance of conflict.

Synergy is hard to develop. Lack of experience and strong cultural biases against group efforts worsen the problem. Groups, like other highly complicated organisms, need time to develop. They need a gestation period to develop interaction, trust, communication, and commitment. No one should expect an easy maturity in groups any more than in young children.

Expensive and time-consuming as it is, building synergetic and collaborative cultures will become essential. Modern problems are too complex and diversified for one man or one discipline. They require a blending of skills and perspectives, and only effective problem-solving units will be able to master them.

Responding to a Turbulent, Uncertain Environment

In the early days of the last war when armaments of all kinds were in short supply, the British, I am told, made use of a venerable field piece that had come down to them from previous generations. The honorable past of this light artillery stretched back, in fact, to the Boer War. In the days of uncertainty after the fall of France, these guns, hitched to trucks, served as useful mobile units in the coast defense. But it was felt that the rapidity of fire could be increased. A time-motion expert was, therefore, called into suggest ways to simplify the firing procedures. He watched one of the gun crews of five men at practice in the field for some time. Puzzled by certain aspects of the procedures, he took some slow-motion pictures of the soldiers performing the loading, aiming, and firing routines.

When he ran those pictures over once or twice, he

noticed something that appeared odd to him. A moment before the firing, two members of the gun crew ceased all activity and came to attention for a three-second interval extending throughout the discharge of the gun. He summoned an old colonel of artillery, showed him the pictures, and pointed out this strange behavior. What, he asked the colonel, did it mean? The colonel, too, was puzzled. He asked to see the pictures again. "Ah," he said when the performance was over, "'I have it. They are holding the horses." (Elting Morison, *Man, Machines and Modern Times*, 1966)

This fable demonstrates nicely the pain with which man accommodates to change. And yet, characteristically and ironically, he continues to seek out new inventions which disorder his serenity and undermine his competence.

One striking index of the rapidity of change—for me, the single, most dramatic index—is the shrinking interval between the time of a discovery and its commercial application. Before World War I, the lag between invention and utilization was 33 years, between World War I and World War II, it was 17 years. After World War II, the interval decreased to about nine years, and if the future can be extrapolated on the basis of the past, by 1970 it will be around five to six years. The transistor was discovered in 1948, and by 1960, 95 percent of all the important equipment and over 50 percent of *all* electronic equipment utilized them in place of conventional vacuum tubes. The first industrial application of computers was as recent as 1956.

Modern organizations, even more than individuals, are acutely vulnerable to the problem of responding flexibly and appropriately to new information. Symptoms of maladaptive responses, at the extremes, are a guarded, frozen, rigidity that denies the presence or avoids the recognition of changes that will result most typically in organizational paralysis; or, at the opposite extreme, an overly receptive, susceptible gullibility to change resulting in a spastic, unreliable faddism. It is obvious that there are times when openness to change is appropriate and other times when it may be disastrous. Organizations, in fact, should reward people who act as counterchange agents to create forces against the seduction of novelty for its own sake.

How can the leadership of these new style organizations create an atmosphere of continuity and stability amidst an environment of change? Whitehead put the problem well:

> The art of society consists first in the maintenance of the symbolic code, and secondly, in the fearlessness of revision . . . Those societies which cannot combine reverance to their symbols with freedom of revision must ultimately decay. . . .

There is no easy solution to the tension between stability and change. We are not yet an emotionally adaptive society, though we are as close to having to become one as any society in history. Elting Morison suggests in his brilliant essay on change that "we may find at least part of our salvation in identifying ourselves with the adaptive process and thus share some of the joy, exuberance, satisfaction, and security . . . to meet . . . changing times."

The remarkable aspect of our generation is its commitment to change in thought and action. Executive leadership must take some responsibility in creating a climate that provides the security to identify with the adaptive process without fear of losing status. Creating an environment that would increase a tolerance for ambiguity and where one can make a virtue out of contingency, rather than one that induces hesitancy and its reckless counter-part, expedience, is one of the most challenging tasks for the new leadership.

Clarity, Commitment, and Consensus

Organizations, like individuals, suffer from "identity crises." They are not only afflictions that attack during adolescence, but chronic states pervading every phase of organizational development. The new organizations we speak of, with their bands of professional problem-solvers, coping within a turbulent environment, are particularly allergic to problems of identity. Professional and regional orientations lead frequently to fragmentation, intergroup conflicts, and power plays and rigid compartmentalization, devoid of any unifying sense of purpose or mission.

The university is a wondrous place for advanced battle techniques, far surpassing their business counterparts in subterfuge and sabotage. Quite often a university becomes a loose collection of competing departments, schools, in-stitutes, committees, centers, programs, largely noncom-municating because of the multiplicity of specialist jar-gons and interests, and held together, as Robert Hutchins once said, chiefly by a central heating system, or as Clark Kerr amended, by questions of what to do about the park-ing problem.

The modern organizations we speak of are composed of men who love independence as fiercely as the ancient Greeks; but it is also obvious that they resist what every Athenian, as a matter of course, gave time and effort for: "building and lifting up the common life."

Thucydides has Pericles saying:

We are a free democracy. . . . We do not allow absorp-tion in our own affairs to interfere with participation in the city's. We regard men who hold aloof from public affairs as useless; nevertheless we yield to none in independence of spirit and complete self-reliance.

A modern version of the same problem (which the Greeks couldn't solve either, despite the lofty prose) has been stated by the president of a large university:

The problem with this institution is that too few people understand or care about the overall goals. Typically they see the world through their own myopic departmental glasses; i.e., too constricted and biased. What we need more of are professional staff who can wear not only their own school or departmental "hat" but the overall university hat.

Specialism, by definition, implies a peculiar slant, a skewed vision of reality. McLuhan tells a good joke on this subject. A tailor went to Rome and managed to get an audience with his Holiness. Upon his return, a friend asked him, "What did the Pope look like?" The tailor answered, "A 41 regular."

Having heard variations of this theme over the years, a number of faculty and administrators, who thought they could "wear the overall university hat" formed what later came to be known as "the HATS group." They came from a variety of departments and hierarchical levels and represented a rough microcosm of the entire university. The HATS group has continued to meet over the past several years and has played an important role in influencing university policy.

There are a number of functions that leadership can perform in addition to developing HATS groups. First, it can identify and support those persons who are "linking pins," individuals with a psychological and intellectual affinity for a number of languages and cultures. Secondly, it can work at the places where the different disciplines and organizations come together (for example, setting up new interdisciplinary programs), in order to create more intergroup give and take.

The third important function for leadership is developing and shaping identity. Organizations, not only the academic disciplines, require philosophers, individuals who can provide articulation between seemingly inimical interests, and who can break down the pseudospecies, transcend vested interests, regional ties, and professional biases. This is precisely what Mary Parker Follett had in mind when she discussed leadership in terms of an ability to bring about a "creative synthesis" between differing codes of conduct.

Chester Barnard in his classic *Functions of the Executive* (1938) recognized this, as well as the personal energy and cost of political process. He wrote, "it seems to me that the struggle to maintain cooperation among men should as surely destroy some men morally as battle destroys some physically."

The Problem of Growth and Decay

For the leader, the organization has to take a conscious responsibility for its own evolution; without a planned methodology and explicit direction, the enterprise will not realize its full potential. For the leader, this is the issue of revitalization and it confronts him with the ultimate challenge: growth or decay.

The challenge for the leader is to develop a climate of inquiry and enough psychological and employment security for continual reassessment and renewal. This task is connected with the leader's ability to collect valid data, feed it back to the appropriate individuals, and develop action planning on the basis of the data. This three-step "action-research" model sounds deceptively simple. In fact, it is difficult. Quite often, the important data cannot be collected by the leader for many obvious reasons. Even when the data are known, there are many organizational short circuits and "dithering devices" that distort and prevent the data from getting to the right places at the right time. And even when data-gathering and feedback are satisfactorily completed, organizational inhibitions may not lead to implementation.

In response to the need for systematic data collection, many organizations are setting up "Institutional Research" centers that act as basic fact-gathering agencies. In some cases, they become an arm of policy-making. Mostly, they see as their prime responsibility the collection and analysis of data that bear on the effectiveness with which the organization achieves its goals.

Fact-gathering, by itself, is rarely sufficient to change attitudes and beliefs and to overcome natural inertia and unnatural resistance to change. Individuals have an awesome capacity to "selectively inattend" to facts that may in their eyes threaten their self-esteem. Facts and reason may be the least potent forms of influence that man possesses.

Some progressive organizations are setting up organizational development departments that attempt to reduce the "implementation gap" between information and new ideas and action. These OD departments become the center for the entire strategic side of the organization, including not only long-run planning, but plans for gaining participation and commitment to the plans. This last step is the most crucial for the guarantee of successful implementation.

In addition to substantive competence and comprehension of both social and technical systems, the new leader will have to possess interpersonal skills, not the least of which is the ability to defer his own immediate desires and gratifications in order to cultivate the talents of others. Let us examine some of the ways leadership can successfully cope with the new organizational patterns.

Understanding the "social territory"

"You gotta know the territory," sang "Professor" Harold Hill to his fellow salesmen in *The Music Man*. The "social territory" encompasses the complex and dynamic interaction of individuals, roles, groups, organizational and cultural systems. Organizations are, of course, legal, political, technical, and economic systems. For our purposes, we will focus on the social system.

Analytic tools, drawn primarily from social psychology and sociology, are available to aid in the understanding of the social territory. But we need more than such tools to augment and implement these understandings. Leadership is as much craft as science. The main instrument or "tool" for the leader-as-a-craftsman is *himself* and how creatively he can use his own personality. This is particularly important for leaders to understand, for, like physicians, they are just as capable of spreading as of curing disease. And again, like the physician, it is important that the leader heed the injunction "heal thyself" so that he does not create pernicious effects unwittingly. Unless the leader understands his actions and effects on others, he may be a "carrier" rather than a solver of problems. Understanding the social territory and how one influences it is related to the "action-research" model of leadership mentioned earlier: 1) collect data, 2) feed it back to appropriate sources, and 3) action-planning. The "hang-up" in most organizations is that people tend to distort and suppress data for fear of real or fancied retaliation. (Samuel Goldwyn, a notorious martinet, called his top staff together after a particularly bad box-office flop and said: "Look, you guys, I want you to tell me exactly what's wrong with this operation and my leadership—even if it means losing your job!")

The Concept of "System-Intervention"

Another aspect of the social territory that has key significance for leadership is the idea of *system*. At least two decades of research have been making this point unsuccessfully. Research has shown that productivity can be modified by what the group thinks important, that training effects fade out and deteriorate if they do not fit the goals of the social system, that group cohesiveness is a powerful motivator, that conflict between units is a major problem in organizations, that individuals take many of their cues and derive a good deal of their satisfaction from their primary work group, that identification with the small work group turns out to be the only stable predictor of productivity, and so on.

The fact that this evidence is so often cited and rarely acted upon leads one to infer that there is some sort of involuntary reflex that makes us locate problems in faulty individuals rather than in malfunctioning social systems. What this irrational reflex is based upon is not altogether clear. But individuals, living amidst complex and subtle organizational conditions, do tend to oversimplify and distort complex realities so that people rather than conditions embody the problem. This tendency toward personalization can be observed in many situations. In international affairs, we blame our troubles with France on deGaulle, or talk sometimes as though we believe that replacing Diem, or Khanh, or Ky will solve our problems with the Saigon government. Other illustrations can be seen when members of organizations take on familial nicknames, such as "Dad,"

"Big Brother," "Man," "Mother Hen," "Dutch Uncle," etc. We can see it in distorted polarizations such as the "good guy" leader who is too trusting, and his "hatchet man" assistant who is really to blame. These grotesques seem to bear such little resemblance to the actual people that one has to ask what psychological needs are being served by this complex labeling and stereotyping.

One answer was hinted at earlier in the Freud quote. He said that work provides an outlet for displacing emotional components onto professional work and the human relations associated with work. If there were no "Big Daddys" or "Queen Bees," we would have to invent them as therapeutic devices to allay anxieties about less romantic, more immediate mothers and fathers, brothers and sisters.

Another reason for this tendency toward personalization is related to the wounded narcissism leaders often suffer. Organizations are big, complex, wondrous—and hamstrung with inertia. Impotence and alienation imprison the best of men, the most glorious of intentions. There is a myth that the higher one goes up the ladder, the more freedom and potency one experiences. In fact, this is frequently not the case, as almost any chief executive will report: the higher he goes the more tethered and bound he may feel by expectations and commitments. In any case, as one gets entrapped by inertia and impotence, it is easier to blame heroes and villains than the system. For if the problems are embroidered into the fabric of the social system, complex as they are, the system can be changed. But if the problems are people, then the endemic lethargy can be explained away by the difficulty—the impossibility—of "changing human nature."

If management insists on personalizing problems that

arise from systems, serious repercussions must result. In the new organizations—where roles will be constantly changing and ambiguous, where changes in one subsystem will clearly affect other subsystems, where diverse activities have to be coordinated and integrated, where individuals work simultaneously in many different jobs and groups—a system viewpoint must be developed. Just as psychotherapists find it difficult to treat a "problem child" without treating the entire family, it will be more difficult to influence individual behavior without working with his particular subsystem. The leader will be compelled to intervene at the system level if the intervention is to last and serve its purpose.

An Agricultural Model of Leadership

I have not found the right word or phrase that accurately portrays the concept of leadership I have in mind—which can be summarized as follows: *an active method for producing conditions where people and ideas and resources can be seeded, cultivated, and integrated to optimum effectiveness and growth.* The phrase "other-directedness," unfortunately, has taken on the negative tone of "exclusively tuned into outside cues." For awhile I thought that "applied biology" might capture the idea, for it connotes an ecological point of view; a process of observation, careful intervention, and organic development. I have also noticed that many biologists and physicians (particularly those physicians who either have no practices or went into public health, psychiatry, or research) are excellent administrators. Socrates used a close and congenial metaphor to symbolize the role of the teacher, the "midwife," someone who helped others to give birth to creations.

The most appropriate metaphor I have found to characterize adaptive leadership is an "agricultural" model.

The leader's job, as I have stated, is to build a climate where growth and development are culturally induced. Roy Ash, an astute industrialist and chairman of Litton Industries, remarked recently, "If the larger corporations, classically viewed as efficient machines rather than hot-houses for fomenting innovation, can become both of these at once, industrial competition will have taken on new dimensions." I think Ash captures exactly the shift in metaphor I am getting at, from a mechanical model to an organic one. Up until very recent times, the metaphor most commonly used to describe power and leadership in organizations derived from Helmholtz's laws of mechanics. Max Weber, who first conceptualized the model of bureaucracy, wrote, "Bureaucracy is like a modern judge who is a vending machine into which the pleadings are inserted along with the fee and which then disgorges the judgment with its reasons mechanically derived from the code."

The language of organizational dynamics in most contemporary writings reflects the machine metaphor: social engineering, equilibrium, friction, resistance, force-field, etc. The vocabulary for adaptive organizations requires an organic metaphor, a description of a *process,* not structural arrangements. This process must include such terms as open, dynamic systems, developmental, organic, adaptive, etc.

All of these strategic and practical considerations lead to a totally new concept of leadership. The pivotal aspect of this concept is that it relies less on the leader's substantive knowledge about a particular topic than it does on the understanding and possession of skills summarized under the agricultural model.

This new concept of leadership embraces four important sets of competencies: 1) knowledge of large, complex human systems; 2) practical theories of intervening and guiding these systems, theories that encompass methods for seeding, nurturing, and integrating individuals and groups; 3) interpersonal competence, particularly the sensitivity to understand the effects of one's own behavior on others and how one's own personality shapes his particular leadership style and value system; and 4) a set of values and competencies which enables one to know when to confront and attack, if necessary, and when to support and provide the psychological safety so necessary for growth.

It is amusing and occasionally frustrating to note that the present view of leadership which I have referred to as an agricultural model, is often construed as "passive" or "weak" or "soft" or more popularly "permissive," and generally dismissed with the same uneasy, patronizing shrug one usually reserves for women who try, however clumsily, to play a man's game. The fact is that the role of leadership described here is clearly more demanding and formidable than any other historical precedent, from king to Pope.

It may be that the common tendency to give this new leadership role such passive and effeminate names betrays the anxiety that many must feel at the final downfall of that distant, stern, strict Victorian father, whose surrogate has led us so often as teacher, military commander, and corporation president. Perhaps that is the only kind of authority we have experienced first hand, or know intimately, or even consider legitimate. But if this new man of power —other-directed and interpersonally competent—takes over the dominant role, as he now seems to be doing, then not only will new myths and archetypes have to substitute for the old, family ones, but new ways—perhaps new legends—will have to be developed to dramatize the rise of new heroes. Let us hope that this new tradition of leadership is not only more potent, but in the long run more gratifying.

July/August 1969

Why All of Us
May Be Hippies Some Day

FRED DAVIS

And thus in love we have declared the purpose of our hearts plainly, without flatterie, expecting love, and the same sincerity from you, without grumbling, or quarreling, being Creatures of your own image and mould, intending no other matter herein, but to observe the Law of righteous action, endeavoring to shut out of the Creation, the cursed thing, called Particular Propriety, which is the cause of all wars, bloud-shed, theft, and enslaving Laws, that hold the people under miserie.

Signed for and in behalf of all the poor oppressed people of England, and the whole world.

Gerrard Winstanley and others
June 1, 1649

This quotation is from the leader of the Diggers, a millenarian sect of communistic persuasion that arose in England at the time of Oliver Cromwell. Today in San Francisco's hippie community, the Haight-Ashbury district, a group of hippies naming themselves after this sect dis-

57

tributes free food to fellow hippies (and all other takers, for that matter) who congregate at about four o'clock every afternoon in the district's Panhandle, an eight-block strip of urban green, shaded by towering eucalyptus trees, that leads into Golden Gate Park to the west. On the corner of a nearby street, the "Hashbury" Diggers operate their Free Store where all—be they hip, straight, hostile, curious, or merely in need—can avail themselves (free of charge, no questions asked) of such used clothing, household articles, books, and second-hand furniture as find their way into the place on any particular day. The Diggers also maintained a large flat in the district where newly arrived or freshly dispossessed hippies could stay without charge for a night, a week, or however long they wished —until some months ago, when the flat was condemned by the San Francisco Health Department. Currently, the Diggers are rehabilitating a condemned skid-row hotel for the same purpose.

Not all of Haight-Ashbury's 7500 hippies are Diggers, although no formal qualifications bar them; nor, in one sense, are the several dozen Diggers hippies. What distinguishes the Diggers—an amorphous, shifting, and sometimes contentious amalgam of ex-political radicals, psychedelic mystics, Ghandians, and Brechtian avant-garde thespians—from the area's "ordinary" hippies is their ideological brio, articulateness, good works, and flair for the dramatic event. (Some are even rumored to be over 30.) In the eyes of many Hashbury hippies, therefore, the Diggers symbolize what is best, what is most persuasive and purposive, about the surrounding, more variegated hippie subculture—just as, for certain radical social critics of the American scene, the hippies are expressing, albeit elliptically, what is best about a seemingly ever-broader segment of American youth: its openness to new experience, puncturing of cant, rejection of bureaucratic regimentation, aversion to violence, and identification with the exploited and disadvantaged. That this is not the whole story barely needs saying. Along with the poetry and flowers, the melancholy smile at passing and ecstatic clasp at greeting, there is also the panicky incoherence of the bad LSD trip, the malnutrition, a startling rise in V.D. and hepatitis, a seemingly phobic reaction to elementary practices of hygiene and sanitation, and—perhaps most disturbing in the long run—a casualness about the comings and goings of human relationships that must verge on the grossly irresponsible.

But, then, social movements—particularly of this expressive-religious variety—are rarely of a piece, and it would be unfortunate if social scientists, rather than inquiring into the genesis, meaning, and future of the hippie movement, too soon joined ranks (as many are likely to, in any case) with solid burghers in an orgy of research into the "pathology" of it all: the ubiquitous drug use (mainly marihuana and LSD, often amphetamines, rarely heroin or other opiates), the easy attitudes toward sex ("If two people are attracted to each other, what better way of showing it than to make love?"), and the mocking hostility toward the middle-class values of pleasure-deferral, material success, and—ultimately—the whole mass-media-glamorized round of chic, deodorized, appliance-glutted suburban existence.

Clearly, despite whatever real or imagined "pathology" middle-class spokesmen are ready to assign to the hippies, it is the middle-class scheme of life that young hippies are reacting against, even though in their ranks are to be found some youth of working-class origin who have never enjoyed the affluence that their peers now so heartily decry.

To adulterate somewhat the slogan of Marshall McLuhan, one of the few non-orientalized intellectuals whom hippies bother to read at all, *the hip scene is the message,* not the elements whence it derives or the meanings that can be assigned to it verbally. (Interestingly, this fusion of disparate classes does not appear to include any significant number of the Negro youths who reside with their families in the integrated Haight-Ashbury district or in the adjoining Negro ghetto, the Fillmore district. By and large, Negroes view with bewilderment and ridicule the white hippies who flaunt, to the extent of begging on the streets, their rejection of what the Negroes have had scant opportunity to attain. What more revealing symbol of the Negro riots in our nation's cities than the carting off of looted TV sets, refrigerators, and washing machines? After all, aren't these things what America is all about?)

But granting that the hippie scene is a reaction to middle-class values, can the understanding of any social movement—particularly one that just in the process of its formation is so fecund of new art forms, new styles of dress and demeanor, and (most of all) new ethical bases for human relationships—ever be wholly reduced to its reactive aspect? As Ralph Ellison has eloquently observed in his critique of the standard sociological explanation of the American Negro's situation, a people's distinctive way of life is never solely a reaction to the dominant social forces that have oppressed, excluded, or alienated them from the larger society. The cumulative process of reaction and counterreaction, in its historical unfolding, creates its own ground for the emergence of new symbols, meanings, purposes, and social discoveries, none of which are ever wholly contained in embryo, as it were, in the conditions that elicited the reaction. It is, therefore, less with an eye toward explaining "how it came to be" than toward explaining what it may betoken of life in the future society that I now want to examine certain facets of the Hashbury hippie subculture. (Of course, very similar youth movements, subcultures, and settlements are found nowadays in many parts of the affluent Western world—Berkeley's Telegraph Avenue teeny-boppers; Los Angeles' Sunset Strippers; New York's East Village hippies; London's mods; Amsterdam's Provos; and the summer *Wandervögel* from all over Europe who chalk the pavement of Copenhagen's main shopping street, the Strøget, and sun themselves on the steps of Stockholm's Philharmonic Hall. What is culturally significant about the Haight-Ashbury hippies is, I would hazard, in general significant about these others as well, with—to be sure—certain qualifications. Indeed, a certain marvelous irony attaches itself to the fact that perhaps the only genuine cross-national culture found in the world today builds on the rag-tag of beards, bare feet, bedrolls, and beads, not on the cultural-exchange programs of governments and universities, or tourism, or—least of all—ladies' clubs' invocations for sympathetic understanding of one's foreign neighbors.)

What I wish to suggest here is that there is, as Max Weber would have put it, an *elective affinity* between prominent styles and themes in the hippie subculture and certain incipient problems of identity, work, and leisure that loom ominously as Western industrial society moves into an epoch of accelerated cybernation, staggering material abundance, and historically-unprecedented mass opportunities for creative leisure and enrichment of the human personality. This is not to say that the latter are the *hidden causes* or tangible *motivating forces* of the former. Rather, the point is that the hippies, in their collective, yet radical, break with the constraints of our present society, are— whether they know it or not (some clearly do intuit a connection)—already rehearsing *in vivo* a number of possible cultural solutions to central life problems posed by the emerging society of the future. While other students of contemporary youth culture could no doubt cite many additional emerging problems to which the hippie subculture is, willy-nilly, addressing itself (marriage and family organization, the character of friendship and personal loyalties, the forms of political participation), space and the kind of observations I have been able to make require that I confine myself to three: the problems of *compulsive consumption,* of *passive spectatorship,* and of the *time-scale of experience.*

What working attitude is man to adopt toward the potential glut of consumer goods that the new technology will make available to virtually all members of the future society? Until now, modern capitalist society's traditional response to short-term conditions of overproduction has been to generate—through government manipulation of fiscal devices—greater purchasing power for discretionary consumption. At the same time, the aim has been to cultivate the acquisitive impulse—largely through mass advertising, annual styling changes, and planned obsolescence—so that, in the economist's terminology, a high level of aggregate demand could be sustained. Fortunately, given the great backlog of old material wants and the technologically-based creation of new wants, these means have, for the most part, worked comparatively well—both for advancing (albeit unequally) the mass standard of living and ensuring a reasonably high rate of return to capital.

But, as Walter Weisskopf, Robert Heilbroner, and other economists have wondered, will these means prove adequate for an automated future society in which the mere production of goods and services might easily outstrip man's desire for them, or his capacity to consume them in satisfying ways? Massive problems of air pollution, traffic congestion, and waste disposal aside, is there no psychological limit to the number of automobiles, TV sets, freezers, and dishwashers that even a zealous consumer can aspire to, much less make psychic room for in his life space? The specter that haunts post-industrial man is that of a near worker-less economy in which most men are constrained, through a variety of economic and political sanctions, to frantically purchase and assiduously use up the cornucopia of consumer goods that a robot-staffed factory system (but one still harnessed to capitalism's rationale of pecuniary profit) regurgitates upon the populace. As far back as the late 1940s sociologists like David Riesman were already pointing to the many moral paradoxes of work, leisure, and interpersonal relations posed by a then only nascent society of capitalist mass abundance. How much more perplexing the paradoxes if, using current technological trends, we extrapolate to the year 2000?

Hippies, originating mainly in the middle classes, have been nurtured at the boards of consumer abundance. Spared their parents' vivid memories of economic depression and material want, however, they now, with what to their elders seems like insulting abandon, declare unshamefacedly that the very quest for "the good things of life" and all that this entails—the latest model, the third car, the monthly credit payments, the right house in the right neighborhood —are a "bad bag." In phrases redolent of nearly all utopian thought of the past, they proclaim that happiness and a meaningful life are not to be found in things, but in the cultivation of the self and by an intensive exploration of inner sensibilities with like-minded others.

Extreme as this antimaterialistic stance may seem, and despite its probable tempering should hippie communities develop as a stable feature on the American landscape, it nonetheless points a way to a solution of the problem of material glut; to wit, the simple demonstration of the ability to live on less, thereby calming the acquisitive frenzy that would have to be sustained, and even accelerated, if the present scheme of capitalist production and distribution were to remain unchanged. Besides such establishments as the Diggers' Free Store, gleanings of this attitude are even evident in the street panhandling that so many hippies engage in. Unlike the street beggars of old, there is little that is obsequious or deferential about their manner. On the contrary, their approach is one of easy, sometimes condescending casualness, as if to say, "You've got more than enough to spare, I need it, so let's not make a degrading charity scene out of my asking you." The story is told in the Haight-Ashbury of the patronizing tourist who, upon being approached for a dime by a hippie girl in her late teens, took the occasion to deliver a small speech on how delighted he would be to give it to her— provided she first told him what she needed it for. Without blinking an eye she replied, "It's my menstrual period and that's how much a sanitary napkin costs."

As social historians are forever reminding us, modern man has—since the beginnings of the industrial revolution —become increasingly a spectator and less a participant. Less and less does he, for example, create or play music, engage in sports, dance or sing; instead he watches professionally-trained others, vastly more accomplished than himself, perform their acts while he, perhaps, indulges in Mitty-like fantasies of hidden graces and talents. Although this bald statement of the spectator thesis has been challenged in recent years by certain social researchers—statistics are cited of the growing numbers taking guitar lessons, buying fishing equipment, and painting on Sunday—

there can be little doubt that "doing" kinds of expressive pursuits, particularly of the collective type, no longer bear the same *integral* relationship to daily life that they once did, or still do in primitive societies. The mere change in how they come to be perceived, from what one does in the ordinary course of life to one's "hobbies," is in itself of profound historical significance. Along with this, the virtuoso standards that once were the exclusive property of small aristocratic elites, rather than being undermined by the oft-cited revolutions in mass communications and mass education, have so diffused through the class structure as to even cause the gifted amateur *at play* to apologize for his efforts with some such remark as, "I only play at it." In short, the cult of professionalism, in the arts as elsewhere, has been institutionalized so intensively in Western society that the ordinary man's sense of expressive adequacy and competence has progressively atrophied. This is especially true of the college-educated, urban middle classes, which —newly exposed to the lofty aesthetic standards of high culture—stand in reverent, if passive, awe of them.

Again, the problem of excessive spectatorship has not proved particularly acute until now, inasmuch as most men have had other time-consuming demands to fill their lives with, chiefly work and family life, leavened by occasional vacations and mass-produced amusements. But what of the future when, according to such social prognosticators as Robert Theobald and Donald Michael, all (except a relatively small cadre of professionals and managers) will be faced with a surfeit of leisure time? Will the mere extension of passive spectatorship and the professional's monopoly of expressive pursuits be a satisfactory solution?

Here, too, hippies are opening up new avenues of collective response to life issues posed by a changing sociotechnological environment. They are doing so by rejecting those virtuoso standards that stifle participation in high culture; by substituting an extravagantly eclectic (and, according to traditional aestheticians, reckless) admixture of materials, styles, and motifs from a great diversity of past and present human cultures; and, most of all, by insisting that every man can find immediate expressive fulfillment provided he lets the socially-suppressed spirit within him ascend into vibrant consciousness. The manifesto is: All men are artists, and who cares that some are better at it than others; we can all have fun! Hence, the deceptively crude antisophistication of hippie art forms, which are, perhaps, only an apparent reversion to primitivism. One has only to encounter the lurid *art nouveau* contortions of the hippie posters and their Beardsleyan exoticism, or the mad mélange of hippie street costume—Greek-sandaled feet peeking beneath harem pantaloons encased in a fringed American Indian suede jacket, topped by pastel floral decorations about the face—or the sitar-whining cacophony of the folk-rock band, to know immediately that one is in the presence of *expressiveness* for its own sake.

In more mundane ways, too, the same readiness to let go, to participate, to create and perform without script or forethought is everywhere evident in the Hashbury. Two youths seat themselves on the sidewalk or in a store entranceway; bent beer can in hand, one begins scratching a bongo-like rhythm on the pavement while the other tattoos a bell-like accompaniment by striking a stick on an empty bottle. Soon they are joined, one by one, by a tambourinist, a harmonica player, a penny-whistler or recorder player, and, of course, the ubiquitous guitarist. A small crowd collects and, at the fringes, some blanket-bedecked boys and girls begin twirling about in movements vaguely resembling a Hindu dance. The wailing, rhythmic beating and dancing, alternately rising to peaks of intensity and subsiding, may last for as little as five minutes or as long as an hour, players and dancers joining in and dropping out as whim moves them. At some point—almost any—a mood takes hold that "the happening is over"; participants and onlookers disperse as casually as they had collected.

Analogous scenes of "participation unbound" are to be observed almost every night of the week (twice on Sunday) at the hippies' Parnassus, the Fillmore Auditorium, where a succession of name folk-rock bands, each more deafening than the one before, follow one another in hour-long sessions. Here, amidst the electric guitars, the electric organs, and the constantly metamorphizing show of lights, one can see the gainly and the graceless, the sylph bodies and rude stompers, the crooked and straight—all, of whatever condition or talent, *dance* as the flickering of a strobe light reduces their figures in silhouette to egalitarian spastic bursts. The recognition dawns that this, at last, is dancing of utterly free form, devoid of fixed sequence or step, open to all and calling for no Friday after-school classes at Miss Martha's or expensive lessons from Arthur Murray. The sole requisite is to tune in, take heart, and let go. What follows must be "beautiful" (a favorite hippie word) because it is *you* who are doing and feeling, not another to whom you have surrendered the muse.

As with folk-rock dancing, so (theoretically, at least) with music, poetry, painting, pottery, and the other arts and crafts: expression over performance, impulse over product. Whether the "straight world" will in time heed this message of the hippies is, to be sure, problematical. Also, given the lavish financial rewards and prestige heaped upon more talented hippie artists by a youth-dominated entertainment market, it is conceivable that high standards of professional performance will develop here as well (listen to the more recent Beatles' recordings), thus engendering perhaps as great a participative gulf between artist and audience as already exists in the established arts. Despite the vagaries of forecasting, however, the hippies—as of now, at least—are responding to the incipient plenitude of leisure in ways far removed from the baleful visions of a Huxley or an Orwell.

In every society, certain activities are required to complete various tasks and to achieve various goals. These activities form a sequence—they may be of short duration and simple linkage (boiling an egg); long duration and complex linkage (preparing for a profession); or a variety of intermediate combinations (planting and harvesting a crop). And the activity sequences needed to complete valued tasks and to achieve valued goals in a society largely determine how the people in that society will subjectively experience *time*.

The distinctive temporal bent of industrial society has been toward the second of these arrangements, long duration and complex linkage. As regards the subjective experience of time, this has meant what the anthropologist Florence Kluckhohn has termed a strong "future orientation" on the part of Western man, a quality of sensibility that radically distinguishes him from his peasant and tribal forebears. The major activities that fill the better part of his life acquire their meaning less from the pleasure they may or may not give at the moment than from their perceived relevance to some imagined future state of being or affairs, be it salvation, career achievement, material success, or the realization of a more perfect social order. Deprived of the pursuit of these temporally distant, complexly modulated goals, we would feel that life, as the man in the street puts it, is without meaning.

This subjective conception of time and experience is, of course, admirably suited to the needs of post-18th century industrial society, needs that include a stable labor force; work discipline; slow and regular accumulation of capital with which to plan and launch new investments and to expand; and long, arduous years of training to provide certain people with the high levels of skill necessary in so many professions and technical fields. If Western man had proved unable to defer present gratifications for future rewards (that is, if he had not been a future-oriented being), nothing resembling our present civilization, as Freud noted, could have come to pass.

Yet, paradoxically, it is the advanced technology of computers and servo-mechanisms, not to overlook nuclear warfare, that industrial civilization has carried us to that is raising grave doubts concerning this temporal ordering of affairs, this optimistic, pleasure-deferring, and magically rationalistic faith in converting present effort to future pay-off. Why prepare, if there will be so few satisfying jobs to prepare for? Why defer, if there will be a superabundance of inexpensively-produced goods to choose from? Why plan, if all plans can disintegrate into nuclear dust?

Premature or exaggerated as these questions may seem, they are being asked, especially by young people. And merely to ask them is to prompt a radical shift in time-perspective—from what *will be* to what *is,* from future promise to present fulfillment, from the mundane discounting of present feeling and mood to a sharpened awareness of their contours and their possibilities for instant alteration. Broadly, it is to invest present experience with a new cognitive status and importance: a lust to extract from the living moment its full sensory and emotional potential. For if the present is no longer to held hostage to the future, what other course than to ravish it at the very instant of its apprehension?

There is much about the hippie subculture that already betokens this alteration of time-perspective and concomitant reconstitution of the experienced self. Hippie argot— some of it new, much of it borrowed with slight connotative changes from the Negro, jazz, homosexual, and addict subcultures—is markedly skewed toward words and phrases in the active present tense: "happening," "where it's at," "turn on," "freak out," "grooving," "mind-blowing, "be-in," "cop out," "split," "drop acid" (take LSD), "put on," "uptight" (anxious and tense), "trip out" (experience the far-out effects of a hallucinogenic drug). The very concept of a happening signifies immediacy: Events are to be actively engaged in, improvised upon, and dramatically exploited for their own sake, with little thought about their origins, duration, or consequences. Thus, almost anything—from a massive be-in in Golden Gate Park to ingesting LSD to a casual street conversation to sitting solitarily under a tree—is approached with a heightened awareness of its happening potential. Similarly, the vogue among Hashbury hippies for astrology, tarot cards, I Ching, and other forms of thaumaturgic prophecy (a hippie conversation is as likely to begin with "What's your birthday?" as "What's your name?") seems to be an attempt to denude the future of its temporal integrity—its unknowability and slow unfoldingness—by fusing it indiscriminately with present dispositions and sensations. The hippie's structureless round-of-day ("hanging loose"), his disdain for appointments, schedules, and straight society's compulsive parceling out of minutes and hours, are all implicated in his intense reverence for the possibilities of the present and uninterest in the future. Few wear watches, and as a colleague who has made a close participant-observer study of one group of hippies remarked, "None of them ever seems to know what time it is."

It is, perhaps, from this vantage point that the widespread use of drugs by hippies acquires its cultural significance, above and beyond the fact that drugs are easily available in the subculture or that their use (especially LSD) has come to symbolize a distinctive badge of membership in that culture. Denied by our Protestant-Judaic heritage the psychological means for experiencing the moment intensively, for parlaying sensation and exoticizing mundane consciousness, the hippie uses drugs where untutored imagination fails. Drugs impart to the present—or so it is alleged by the hippie psychedelic religionists—an aura of aliveness, a sense of union with fellow man and nature, which—we have been taught—can be apprehended, if not in the afterlife that few modern men still believe in, then only after the deepest reflection and self-knowledge induced by protracted experience.

A topic of lively debate among hippie intellectuals is whether drugs represent but a transitory phase of the hippie subculture to be discarded once other, more self-generating, means are discovered by its members for extracting consummatory meaning from present time, or whether drugs are the *sine qua non* of the subculture. Whatever the case, the hippies' experiment with ways to recast our notions of time and experience is deserving of close attention.

As of this writing, it is by no means certain that Haight-Ashbury's "new community," as hippie spokesmen like to call it, can survive much beyond early 1968. Although the "great summer invasion" of émigré hippies fell far short of the 100,000 to 500,000 forecast, the influx of youth from California's and the nation's metropolitan suburbs was, despite considerable turnover, large enough to place a severe strain on the new community's meager resources. "Crash pads" for the night were simply not available in sufficient quantity; the one daily meal of soup or stew served free by the Diggers could hardly appease youthful appetites; and even the lure of free love, which to young minds might be construed as a substitute for food, tarnished for many—boys outnumbered girls by at least three to one, if not more. Besides, summer is San Francisco's most inclement season, the city being shrouded in a chilling, wind-blown fog much of the time. The result was hundreds of youths leading a hand-to-mouth existence, wandering aimlessly on the streets, panhandling, munching stale doughnuts, sleeping in parks and autos and contracting virulent upper-respiratory infections. In this milieu cases of drug abuse, notably involving Methedrine and other "body-wrecking" amphetamines, have showed an alarming increase, beginning about mid-summer and continuing up to the present. And, while the city fathers were not at first nearly so repressive as many had feared, they barely lifted a finger to ameliorate the situation in the Haight-Ashbury. Recently, however, with the upcoming city elections for Mayor and members of the Board of Supervisors, they have given evidence of taking a "firmer" attitude toward the hippies: Drug arrests are on the increase, many more minors in the area are being stopped for questioning and referral to juvenile authorities, and a leading Haight Street hippie cultural establishment, the Straight Theatre, has been denied a dance permit.

It has not, therefore, been solely the impact of sheer numbers that has subjected the new community to a difficult struggle for survival. A variety of forces, internal and external, appear to have conjoined to crush it. To begin with, there is the hippies' notorious, near-anarchic aversion to sustained and organized effort toward reaching some goal. Every man "does his own thing for as long as he likes" until another thing comes along to distract or delight him, whereupon the hippie ethos enjoins him to drop the first thing. (Shades of the early, utopian Karl Marx: ". . . in the communist society it [will be] possible for me to do this today and that tomorrow, to hunt in the morning, to fish in the afternoon, to raise cattle in the evening, to be a critic after dinner, just as I feel at the moment; without ever being a hunter, fisherman, herdsman, or critic." From *The German Ideology.*) Even with such groups as the Diggers, projects are abandoned almost as soon as they are begun. One of the more prominent examples: An ongoing pastoral idyll of summer cultural happenings, proclaimed with great fanfare in May by a group calling itself the Council for the Summer of Love, was abandoned in June when the Council's leader decided one morning to leave town. Add to this the stalling and ordinance-juggling of a city bureaucracy reluctant to grant hippies permits and licenses for their pet enterprises, and very little manages to get off the ground. With only a few notable exceptions, therefore, like the Haight-Ashbury Free Medical Clinic, which—though closed temporarily—managed through its volunteer staff to look after the medical needs of thousands of hippies during the summer, the new community badly failed to provide for the hordes of youth drawn by its paeans of freedom, love, and the new life. Perhaps there is some ultimate wisdom to "doing one's own thing"; it was, however, hardly a practical way to receive a flock of kinsmen.

Exacerbating the "uptightness" of the hippies is a swelling stream of encounters with the police and courts, ranging from panhandling misdemeanors to harboring runa-

way minors ("contributing to the delinquency of a minor")
to, what is most unnerving for hip inhabitants, a growing
pattern of sudden mass arrests for marihuana use and possession in which as many as 25 youths may be hauled off
in a single raid on a flat. (Some hippies console themselves
with the thought that if enough middle-class youths get
"busted for grass," such a hue and cry will be generated in
respectable quarters that the marihuana laws will soon be
repealed or greatly liberalized.) And, as if the internal
problems of the new community were not enough, apoca-
lyptic rumors sprung up, in the wake of the Newark and
Detroit riots, that "the Haight is going to be burned to
the ground" along with the adjoining Fillmore Negro
ghetto. There followed a series of ugly street incidents between blacks and whites—assaults, sexual attacks, window
smashings—which palpably heightened racial tensions and
fed the credibility of the rumors.

Finally, the area's traffic-choked main thoroughfare,
Haight Street, acquired in the space of a few months so
carnival and Dantesque an atmosphere as to defy description. Hippies, tourists, drug peddlers, Hell's Angels,
drunks, speed freaks (people high on Methedrine), pan-
handlers, pamphleteers, street musicians, crackpot evange-
lists, photographers, TV camera crews, reporters (domestic and foreign), researchers, ambulatory schizophre-
nics, and hawkers of the underground press (at least four
such papers are produced in the Haight-Ashbury alone)
jostled, put-on, and taunted one another through a din
worthy of the Tower of Babel. The street-milling was in-
cessant, and all heads remained cocked for "something to
happen" to crystallize the disarray. By early summer, so
repugnant had this atmosphere become for the "old" hippies (those residing there before—the origins of Hashbury's new community barely go back two years) that

many departed; those who remained did so in the rapidly fading hope that the area might revert to its normal state of abnormality following the expected post-Labor Day exodus of college and high-school hippies. And, while the exodus of summer hippies has indeed been considerable, the consensus among knowledgeable observers of the area is that it has not regained its former, less frenetic, and less disorganized ambience. The transformations wrought by the summer influx—the growing shift to Methedrine as *the* drug of choice, the more general drift toward a wholly drug-oriented subculture, the appearance of hoodlum and thrill-seeking elements, the sleazy tourist shops, the racial tensions—persist, only on a lesser scale.

But though Haight-Ashbury's hippie community may be destined to soon pass from the scene, the roots upon which it feeds run deep in our culture. These are not only of the long-term socio-historic kind I have touched on here, but of a distinctly contemporary character as well, the pain and moral duplicity of our Vietnam involvement being a prominent wellspring of hippie alienation. As the pressures mount on middle-class youth for ever greater scholastic achievement (soon a graduate degree may be mandatory for middle-class status, as a high-school diploma was in the 1940s), as the years of adolescent dependence are further prolonged, and as the accelerated pace of technological change aggravates the normal social tendency to intergenerational conflict, an increasing number of young people can be expected to drop out, or opt out, and drift into the hippie subculture. It is difficult to foresee how long they will remain there and what the consequences for later stages of their careers will be, inasmuch as insufficient time has passed for even a single age cohort of hippies to make the transition from early to middle adulthood. However, even among those youths who "remain in" conventional society in some formal sense, a very large number can be expected to hover so close to the margins of hippie subculture as to have their attitudes and outlooks substantially modified. Indeed, it is probably through some such muted, gradual, and indirect process of social conversion that the hippie subculture will make a lasting impact on American society, if it is to have any at all.

At the same time, the hippie rebellion gives partial, as yet ambiguous, evidence of a massiveness, a universality, and a density of existential texture, all of which promise to transcend the narrowly-segregated confines of age, occupation, and residence that characterized most bohemias of the past (Greenwich Village, Bloomsbury, the Left Bank). Some hippie visionaries already compare the movement to Christianity sweeping the Roman Empire. We cannot predict how far the movement can go toward enveloping the larger society, and whether as it develops it will—as have nearly all successful social movements—significantly compromise the visions that animate it with the practices of the reigning institutional system. Much depends on the state of future social discontent, particularly within the middle classes, and on the viable political options governments have for assuaging this discontent. Judging, however, from the social upheavals and mass violence of recent decades, such options are, perhaps inevitably, scarce indeed. Just possibly, then, by opting out and making their own kind of cultural waves, the hippies are telling us more than we can now imagine about our future selves.

December 1967

How Community Mental Health Stamped Out the Riots (1968-1978)

KENNETH KENISTON

One day, after I gave a lecture in a course on social and community psychiatry, a student asked me whether I thought community mental-health workers would eventually be asked to assume policing functions. I assured him that I thought this very unlikely, and thought no more about it.

That night I had the following dream: I was sitting on the platform of a large auditorium. In the audience were thousands of men and women, some in business clothes, others in peculiar blue and white uniforms that seemed a cross between medical and military garb. I glanced at the others on the platform: Many wore military uniforms. Especially prominent was a tall, distinguished, lantern-jawed general, whose chest was covered with battle ribbons and on whose arm was a blue and white band.

The lights dimmed; I was pushed to my feet and toward the podium. Before me on the lectern was a neatly-typed

*manuscript. Not knowing what else to do, I found myself
beginning to read from it. . . .*

Ladies and Gentlemen: It is a pleasure to open this Eighth
Annual Meeting of the Community Mental Health Organization, and to welcome our distinguished guests: the re-
cently-appointed Secretary for International Mental Health,
General Westmoreland [loud applause], and the Secretary
for Internal Mental Health, General Walt [applause].

This year marks the tenth anniversary of the report of
the First National Advisory Commission on Civil Disorders.
And this meeting of representatives of 3,483 Community
Mental Health Centers, 247 Remote Therapy Centers, and
45 Mobile Treatment Teams may provide a fitting occasion
for us to review the strides we have made in the past decade,
and to contemplate the greater tasks that lie before us. For
it was in the past decade, after all, that the Community
Mental Health movement proved its ability to deal with the
problem of urban violence, and it is in the next decade that
the same approaches must be adapted to the other urgent
mental-health problems of our society and the world.

In my remarks here, I will begin with a review of the
progress of the past decade. Arbitrarily, I will divide the
years since 1968 into three stages: the phase of preparation;
the phase of total mobilization; and the mop-up phase that
we are now concluding.

In retrospect, the years from 1968 to 1970 can be seen
as the time of preparation for the massive interventions that
have since been made. On the one hand, the nation was
faced with mounting urban unrest, especially among disadvantaged sectors of the inner city, unrest that culminated
in the riots of 1969 and 1970, in which property damage
of more than 20 billion dollars was wrought, and in which
more than 5,000 individuals (including 27 policemen,

National Guardsmen, and firemen) were killed. Yet in retrospect, the seeds of "Operation Inner City" were being developed even during this period. As early as 1969, the Cannon Report—a joint product of Community Mental Health workers and responsible leaders of the white and black communities—suggested that (1) the propensity to violence was but a symptom of underlying social and psychological pathology; (2) massive federal efforts must be made to identify the individual and societal dysfunctions that produce indiscriminate protest, and (3) more effective methods must be developed for treating the personal and group disorganization that produces unrest.

From 1968 to 1970, a series of research studies and demonstration projects developed the basic concepts that were implemented in later years. Indeed, without this prior theoretical work by interdisciplinary teams of community psychiatrists, sociologists, social workers, and police officials, Operation Inner City would never have been possible. I need recall only a few of the major contributions: the concept of "aggressive alienation," used to characterize the psychosocial disturbance of a large percentage of inner-city dwellers; McFarland's seminal work on urban disorganization, personal pathology, and aggressive demonstrations; the development, on a pilot basis, of new treatment systems like the "total saturation approach," based upon the concept of "antidotal (total) therapy"; and the recognition of the importance of the "reacculturation experience" in treating those whose personal pathology took the form of violence-proneness. Equally basic theoretical contributions were made by those who began to investigate the relationship between aggressiveness, alienation, and antisocietal behavior in other disturbed sections of the population, such as disacculturated intellectuals and students.

After the riots of 1969, rising public indignation over the senseless slaughter of thousands of Americans and the wanton destruction of property led President Humphrey to create the Third Presidential Task Force on Civil Disorders. After six months of almost continuous study, Task Force chairman Ronald Reagan recommended that massive federal intervention, via the Community Mental Health Centers, be the major instrument in action against violence. Portions of this report still bear quoting: "The experience of the past five years has shown that punitive and repressive intervention aggravates rather than ameliorates the violence of the inner city. It is now amply clear that urban violence is more than sheer criminality. The time has come for America to heed the findings of a generation of research: *inner-city violence is a product of profound personal and social pathology. It requires treatment rather than punishment, rehabilitation rather than imprisonment.*"

The report went on: "The Community Mental Health movement provides the best available weapon in the struggle against community sickness in urban America. The existence of 967 Community Mental Health Centers (largely located in communities with high urban density), the concentration of professional and para-professional mental-health workers in these institutions, and their close contact with the mood and hopes of their inner-city catchment areas all indicate that community mental health should be the first line of attack on urban unrest."

In the next months, an incensed Congress, backed by an outraged nation, passed the first of the series of major bills that led to the creation of Operation Inner City, under the joint auspices of the Department of Health, Education, and Welfare and what was then still called the Department of Defense. Despite the heavy drains on the national economy

made by American involvement in Ecuador, Eastern Nigeria, and Pakistan, five billion dollars were appropriated
the first year, with steadily increasing amounts thereafter.

As the concept of urban pathology gained acceptance,
police officials referred those detained during urban riots
not to jails but to local Community Mental Health Centers.
Viewing urban violence as a psychosocial crisis made possible the application of concepts of "crisis therapy" to the
violence-ridden inner-city dweller. As predicted, early researchers found very high levels of psychopathology in
those referred for treatment, especially in the form of ag-
gravated aggressive-alienation syndrome.

But it was obviously not enough to treat violence only
in its acute phase. Precritical intervention and preventive
rehabilitation were also necessary. So city law-enforcement
officials and mental-health workers began cooperating in
efforts to identify those people whose behavior, group-
membership patterns, and utterances gave evidence of the
prodrome (early symptoms) of aggressive alienation. New
statutes passed by Congress in 1971 empowered mental-
health teams and local authorities to require therapy of those
identified as prodromally violent. In defending this bill in
Congress against the congressional group that opposed it
on civil-libertarian grounds, Senator Murphy of California
noted the widespread acceptance of the principle of compulsory inoculation, mandatory treatment for narcotics ad-
dicts, and hospitalization of the psychotic. "Urban violence,"
he noted, "is no different from any other illness: The welfare of those afflicted requires that the public accept responsibility for their prompt and effective treatment."

Mental-health workers, with legal power to institute
therapy, and in collaboration with responsible political and
law-enforcement authorities, were finally able to implement

the Total Saturation Approach in the years from 1972 to the present. Employing local citizens as "pathology detectors," Community Mental Health teams made massive efforts to detect all groups and individuals with prodromes of violence, or a predisposition to *advocate* violence. In many communities, the incidence of prepathological conditions was almost perfectly correlated with racial origin; hence, massive resources were funneled into these communities in particular to immediately detect and help those afflicted.

At this point, it became evident that programs attempting to treat inner-city patients still remaining in the same disorganized social environment that had originally contributed to their pathology were not entirely successful. It was only in 1971, with Rutherford, Cohen, and Robinson's now classic study, "Relapse Rates in Seven Saturation Projects: a Multi-Variate Analysis," that it was finally realized that short-term, total-push therapies were not effective in the long run. As the authors pointed out, "The reentry of the cured patient into the pathogenic disacculturating community clearly reverses *all* the therapeutic gains of the in-patient phase."

Armed with the Rutherford study, Congress in 1972 passed a third legislative landmark, the Remote Therapy Center Act. Congress—recognizing that prolonged reacculturative experience in a psychologically healthy community (antidotal therapy) was often necessary for the permanent recompensation of deep-rooted personality disorders—authorized the construction of 247 centers, largely in the Rocky Mountain Region, each with a capacity of 1,000 patients. The old Department of Defense (now the Department of International Mental Health) cooperated by making available the sites used in World War II for the relocation of Japanese-Americans. On these salubrious sites, the network of Remote Treatment Centers has now been constructed. Although the stringent security arrangements necessary in such centers have been criticized, the retreats now constitute one of our most effective attacks upon the problem of urban mental illness.

The gradual reduction in urban violence, starting in 1973, cannot be attributed to any single factor. But perhaps one idea played the decisive role. During this period mental-health workers began to realize that earlier approaches, which attempted to ameliorate the objective, physical, or legal conditions under which inner-city dwellers lived, were not only superficial, but were themselves a reflection of serious psychopathology. Reilly, Bernitsky, and O'Leary's now classic study of ex-patients of the retreats established the correlation between a patient's relapse into violence and his preoccupation with what the investigators termed "objectivist" issues: housing, sanitation, legal rights, jobs, education, medical care, and so on.

Two generations ago Freud taught us that what matters most is not objective reality, but the way it is interpreted by the individual. Freud's insight has finally been perceived in its true light—as an attitude essential for healthy functioning. The fact that previous programs of civil rights, slum clearance, legal reforms, and so on, succeeded only in aggravating violence now became fully understandable. Not only did these programs fail to take account of the importance of basic attitudes and values in determining human behavior—thus treating symptoms rather than underlying psychological problems—but, by encouraging objectivism, they directly *undermined* the mental health of those exposed to these programs. Today's mental-health workers recognize objectivism as a prime symptom of individual and community dysfunction, and move swiftly and effectively to institute therapy.

The final step in the development of a community mental-health approach to violence came with the development of the Mobile Treatment ("Motreat") Team. In 1972 the Community Mental Health authorities set up a series of 45 Motreat Teams, organized on a regional basis and consisting of between 500 and 1,000 carefully selected and trained Community Mental Health workers. These heroic groups, wearing their now familiar blue and white garb, were ready on a standby basis to move into areas where violence threatened. Given high mobility by the use of armed helicopters, trained in crisis intervention and emergency treatment, and skilled in the use of modern psychopharmacological sprays and gases, the Motreat Teams have now proved their effectiveness. On numerous occasions during the past years, they have been able to calm an agitated population, to pinpoint the antisocial-violence leaders and refer them for therapy, and thus to lay the basis for society's prompt return to healthy functioning. The architects of the Mobile Treatment Team found that many of their most important insights were obtained from professionals in the field of law enforcement and national defense—more evidence of the importance of interdisciplinary cooperation.

As you all know, the past four years have been years of diminishing urban violence, years when the Community Mental Health movement has received growing acclaim for its success in dealing with social and individual pathology, years when the early criticism of the Community Mental Health movement by the "liberal coalition" in Congress has diminished, largely because the members of that coalition have not been reelected. Today, the Community Mental Health movement has the virtually undivided support of the nation, regardless of political partisanship. The original federal target of 2,800 Community Mental Health Centers has been increased to more than 5,000; the principles of Community Mental Health have been extended from the limited "catchment area" concept to the more relevant concept of "target groups" and beyond; and the Community Mental Health movement faces enormous new challenges.

But before considering the challenges that lie ahead, let us review what we have learned theoretically during the past decade.

Doubtless the most important insight was the awareness that *violence and antisocial behavior are deeply rooted in individual and social pathology,* and must be treated as such. We have at last been able to apply the insights of writers, historians, sociologists, and psychologists of the 1950s and 1960s to a new understanding of black character. The black American—blighted by the deep scars and legacies of his history, demoralized by what Stanley Elkins described as the concentration-camp conditions of slavery, devitalized by the primitive, impulse ridden, and fatherless black families so brilliantly described by Daniel Moynihan —is the helpless victim of a series of deep deprivations that almost inevitably lead to intra-psychic and social pathology. Moreover, we have begun to understand the communicational networks and group-pathological processes that spread alienation and violence from individual to individual, and that make the adolescent especially prone to succumb to the aggressive-alienation syndrome. To be sure, this view was contradicted by the report that many of the advocates of violence—the leaders of the now outlawed black-power group and its precursors, SNCC and CORE—came from relatively nondeprived backgrounds. But later researchers have shown that the virus of aggressive alienation is communicated even within apparently intact families. As Rosen-baum and Murphy put it in a recent review paper, "We have learned that social pathology is no less infectious than the black plague."

Another major theoretical contribution has come from our *redefinition of the concept of community*. As the first Community Mental Health Centers were set up, "community" was defined as a geographically limited catchment area, often heterogeneous in social class, ethnicity, and race. But the events of the last decade have made it amply clear that we cannot conceive of the community so narrowly. The artificial boundaries of the catchment area do not prevent the transmission of social pathology across these boundaries; indeed, efforts to prevent personal mobility and communication between catchment areas proved difficult to implement without an anxiety-provoking degree of coercion. It became clear that cutting across catchment areas were certain pathogenic "target groups" in which the bacillus of social pathology was most infectious. Recognition of the target-group concept of community was the theoretical basis for much recent legislation. Rarely have the findings of the behavioral sciences been translated so promptly into enlightened legislation [applause].

This recognition of the too-narrow definition of "community" led to the creation of the Remote Treatment Centers. True, removing the mentally ill from the violence-prone target groups has not solved the problem completely. But the creation of total therapeutic communities in distant parts of the country has had a salubrious and calming effect on the mental health of the groups the patients came from.

It has also become clear that Community Mental Health efforts aimed solely at the disadvantaged are, by their very nature, limited in effectiveness. The suppression of pathology in one group may paradoxically be related to its sudden emergence in others. Stated differently, pathology moves through the entire community, although it tends to be concentrated during any given period in certain target groups. The international events of the past decade, the appearance of comparable psychopathology in Ecuador, Eastern Nigeria, Pakistan, Thailand, and a variety of other countries, raise the question of whether it is possible to have mental health in one country alone.

Another crucial theoretical advance has been the concept of *total therapy*. Patients and groups must be treated *before* symptoms become acute, because the infectiousness of social pathology increases during the acute phase. What has been termed the "pathology multiplier effect" has been widely recognized: This means that it is essential to prevent the formation of pathologically-interacting groups, especially when organized around societally disruptive objectivist issues like black power, civil rights, or improvement in living conditions. Furthermore, crisis intervention must be supplemented by *prolonged aftercare,* particularly for those whose involvement in violence has been most intense. Of the many post-rehabilitation followup methods attempted, two of the most effective have been the incorporation of rehabilitated patients into mental-health teams working in localities other than their own, and the new programs of aftercare involving the continuing rehabilitation of discharged patients in such challenging areas as Ecuador, Eastern Nigeria, and Pakistan. You are all familiar with the many glowing tributes to this aftercare program recently released by International Mental Health Secretary Westmoreland [applause].

The past decade has also demonstrated beyond doubt the

importance of *inter-agency and inter-disciplinary collabora-tion.* The effectiveness of such collaboration has shown how unfounded were the concerns of the First Joint Commission on Mental Health over inadequate manpower. In large measure because of better and better relationships between mental-health workers, law-enforcement agencies, local civic authorities, the Department of International Mental Health, the National Guard, the Air Force, and other community agencies, radically new patterns of recruitment into the mental-health professions have been established. Indeed, in many communities effective mental-health efforts have permitted a major reduction in the size of law-enforcement authorities, and the training of a whole new group of para-professionals and sub-professionals who, a decade ago, would have entered law-enforcement agencies.

But lest we become complacent about our accomplishments, let me remind you of the many theoretical problems, difficulties, and challenges that lie before us.

Our program has not been without its critics and detractors, and there is much to be learned from them. To be sure, many of the early criticisms of our work can now be understood either as the result of inadequate understanding of the behavioral sciences, or as symptoms of the objectivist social-pathological process itself. In the years before the liberal coalition became moribund, many so-called civil-libertarian critics persisted in ignoring the humanitarian aspects of our program, focusing instead upon the 19th-century concept of civil rights. The political ineffectuality of this group, coupled with the speed with which many of its leaders have recently been reacculturated, suggests the limitations of this viewpoint.

But even within our own midst we have had critics and detractors. We are all familiar with the unhappy story of the American Psychoanalytic Association, which continued its criticisms of our programs until its compulsory incorporation last year into the Community Mental Health Organization. What we must learn from these critics is how easy it is for even the most apparently dedicated mental-health workers to lose sight of broader societal goals, neglecting the population and the societal matrix in a misguided attachment to outmoded concepts of individuality, "reality factors," and "insight therapy."

In my remarks so far, I have emphasized our theoretical and practical progress. But those of us who were involved in the Community Mental Health movement from its beginnings in the early 1960s must remind others that almost all of the major concepts that underlie the progress of the past decade were already in existence in 1968. Even a decade ago, the most advanced workers in the field of community health *knew* that crisis intervention was not enough, and were developing plans for preventive intervention and extensive aftercare. Furthermore, many of the most important concepts in this field derived from researches done by Freud, Anna Freud, Moynihan, Caplan, Gruenberg, Keniston, and others. Even the concept of aggressive alienation itself is based on earlier research on alienation done, not in the inner city, but amongst talented college students. Thus, our enthusiasm for the progress of the past decade must be tempered with humility and a sense of indebtedness to those in the pre-Community Mental Health era.

Furthermore, humility is called for because of the many questions whose answers have evaded our search. I will cite but one of the most important: the problem of therapeutic failure.

We have much to learn from our failures, perhaps more than from our numerous successes. With some patients, even repeated rehabilitation and maintenance on high doses of long-acting tranquilizers have failed to produce a complete return to pro-social functioning. And the uncooperativeness of the government of Canada has made it extremely difficult to reach those unsuccessfully treated patients who have evaded our detection networks and fled north. Since the Canadian government is unwilling to extradite the large numbers of mentally ill who have flocked to Canadian urban centers, we must support the recent proposal of Secretary Westmoreland that we persuade foreign governments to institute their own programs of Community Mental Health, with the close collaboration and support of American advisors. Indeed, the currently strained relations between Canada and the United States raise a series of far more profound questions, to which I will return in a moment.

Rather than list the many other important research issues that confront us, let me turn to our greatest challenge—the definition of new target groups, and the need to broaden still further the concept of community.

In our focus upon the more visible problems of urban violence, we have neglected other target groups of even greater pathological potential. These new target groups are not always easy to define precisely; but there is a clear consensus that high priority on the list of future targets must be given to college students, to intellectuals with no firm ties to the community, and to disacculturated members of certain ethnico-religious groups who retain close ties with non-American communities.

The passage last year of the College Developmental Act enables us at last to apply to the college-age group the techniques so successfully used in the inner city. This act will enable the setting up of college mental-health centers with a strong community approach. One of the particular strengths of this law should be underlined here: It enables us to treat not only the college student himself, but his professors and mentors, from whom—as recent studies have shown—much of his antisocial acculturation springs.

In our continuing work with new target groups, however, we must not lose sight of certain basic principles. For one, the target-group approach is by its very nature limited. Our practical resources are still so small that we must single out only certain target groups for special interventions. But this should not obscure our long-range goal: nothing less than a society in which all men and women are guaranteed mental health by simple virtue of their citizenship. Thus, the entire community must be our target; we must insist upon *total mental health* from the womb to the grave [applause].

Yet our most serious challenge lies not in America, but outside of our national boundaries. For it has become obvious that the concept of "mental health in one nation" is not tenable. We are surrounded by a world in which the concepts of Community Mental Health have had regrettably little impact. Recent studies conducted by the Department of International Mental Health in Ecuador, Eastern Nigeria, and Thailand have shown an incidence of individual and collective psychopathology even higher than that found in American cities ten years ago. The link between objectivism and violence, first established in America, has been repeatedly shown to exist in other cultures as well. Even young Americans serving abroad with the Overseas Mental Health Corps have been exposed to objectivist influences in these countries that have made their renewed rehabilitation necessary, whether on the battlefield or in the special rehabilitation centers back home.

But it should not be thought that the primary argument against mental health in only one country is mere expediency. Our responsibilities as the most powerful and mentally healthy nation in the world are of a therapeutic nature. Were it simply a matter of expediency, the closing of the Canadian and Mexican borders has shown that it is possible to limit the exodus of non-reacculturated Americans to the merest trickle. Nor would sheer expediency alone justify our involvement, at a heavy price in materials and men, in the mental health struggles of Ecuador, Eastern Nigeria, and Thailand. It is not expediency but our therapeutic commitment to the mental health of our fellow men—regardless of race, color, nationality, and creed—that argues against the concept of mental health in only one nation.

Thus, our greatest challenge is the struggle to create a mentally healthy world. Happy historical accident has given American society a technology and an understanding of human behavior sufficiently advanced to bring about the profound revolution in human behavior that men from Plato's time onward have dreamed of. The lessons of Operation Inner City will continue to be of the utmost importance: the concepts of total saturation, remote therapy, and mandatory treatment; the realization of the close link between objectivism and psychopathology; the need for the closest interdisciplinary cooperation. Already, plans evolved by the Department of International Mental Health and this Community Mental Health Organization call for the international deployment of Mobile Treatment Teams and Overseas Mental Health Corps volunteers, some operating with the assistance of local governments, others courageously risking their lives in communities where pathology has infiltrated even the highest levels of governmental authority. In the years to come, the challenges will be great, the price will be large, and the discouragements will be many. But of one thing there can be no doubt: The Community Mental Health movement will play a leading role in our progress toward a mentally healthy society at the head of a mentally healthy world [applause]. . . .

I stepped back from the podium and tripped. Many hands reached to pull me to my feet. I cried out and awoke to find my wife shaking me. "You've been dreaming and mumbling in your sleep for hours," she said, "and you're feverish." The thermometer revealed a temperature of 103 degrees. I was in bed for several days with a rather severe virus—which, doubtless, explains my dream.

July/August 1968

Commentaries on
Report from Iron Mountain

In August of 1963, if we can believe Leonard C. Lewin, a Special Study Group was set up, under Government auspices and with melodramatic secrecy, in order

1. to determine what problems the United States would face if permanent peace broke out; and
2. to draw up a program to deal with these problems.

The Study Group's sponsor was probably an *ad hoc* Government committee at, or near, the cabinet level. Included among the Group's 15 members were an economist, a sociologist, a cultural anthropologist, a psychologist and a psychiatrist, and one literary critic. The 15 met once a month, usually for two days, over a period of two and a half years, the first and final meetings being held in an underground nuclear shelter inside Iron Mountain, in upstate New York (near war-gamer Herman Kahn's Hudson Institute). A report was unanimously agreed upon, then submitted to the Government "interagency committee," along with an urgent recommendation that its contents be kept secret.

There the matter rested—until winter 1966, when a member of the Study Group, "John Doe," came to New York, looked up Leonard Lewin, and handed him a copy of the report, explaining that while he himself accepted all of the *Report*'s conclusions, he also strongly believed that its findings should be made public. Lewin promptly found a publisher, wrote an introduction, included an interview with John Doe, and refused to say another word about the report's origins.

Report from Iron Mountain on the Possibility and Desirability of Peace, with Introductory Material by Leonard C. Lewin (The Dial Press, New York, 1967) says, in essence, that while permanent peace may be possible, it probably would not be desirable. To quote the *Report*: "It is uncertain, at this time, whether peace will ever be possible. It is far more questionable, by the objective standard of continued social survival rather than that of emotional pacifism, that it would be desirable even if it were demonstrably attainable."

Peace, the *Report* concludes, is hell. If society is to remain stable, wars must continue. "War itself is the basic social system, within which other secondary modes of social organization conflict or conspire." The indispensable functions that war and war preparedness serve are assigned to various categories, perhaps the key ones being economic, political, sociological, and ecological.

1. *Economic.* Military spending, by virtue of its independence from the normal supply-demand econ-

omy, acts as a balance wheel. "It is, and has been, the essential economic stabilizer of modern societies." Among possible substitutes offered are a comprehensive social-welfare program; a fantastically elaborate disarmament-inspection system; and an even more enormous investment in space research. Social-welfare programs, however, would not, in the long run, eat up enough resources, and in addition would not remain very long outside the normal economy. A disarmament-inspection system would also not prove "wasteful" enough, and would be incongruous in a world permanently at peace. Space-research programs, the *Report* decides, appear to be the only realistic substitute. (It is the *only* substitute the Study Group warmly endorses.)

2. *Political.* It is only because of the threat of war that individual nations, and stable governments, can exist. ". . . 'war' is virtually synonymous with nationhood. The elimination of war implies the inevitable elimination of national sovereignty and the traditional nation-state." Furthermore, military spending serves to keep a certain portion of the population poor, thus maintaining "necessary class distinctions" and a ready supply of unskilled labor. As a possible substitute, new external enemies might be created—like invaders from outer space, "fictitious alternate enemies," or air and water pollution (which would have to be deliberately intensified). According to the *Report,* only the creation of "fictitious alternate enemies" offers any promise.

3. *Sociological.* The army and the draft serve to remove antisocial members from society. War itself catharsizes aggressive impulses. And the existence of an external menace induces citizens to become patriotic and subservient to the state. "Allegiance requires a

cause; a cause requires an enemy." Possible substitutes: programs like the Peace Corps; "Socially oriented blood games"; and "A modern, sophisticated form of slavery." Of the substitutes, only slavery, the *Report* concludes, may prove "efficient" and "flexible."

4. *Ecological.* War has been the chief evolutionary mechanism for maintaining a proper balance between the population and the supplies the population needs to survive. Here, at least, war has a drawback: It is not eugenic. Nuclear wars, for example, kill off the superior as well as the inferior. A possible substitute *and* improvement: ". . . a universal requirement that procreation be limited to the products of artificial insemination," along with "A comprehensive program of applied eugenics."

What the *Report* does, then, is to legitimize war. The Special Study Group's key conclusion is: "If it were necessary at this moment to opt irrevocably for the retention or dissolution of the war system, common prudence would dictate the former course."

The bulk of the available evidence suggests that the book is a hoax. As for the perpetrator, nominees have included Richard Rovere, John Kenneth Galbraith (who told *Trans-action,* archly, "If I had been a member of the Study Group, I would have been sworn to secrecy"), Kenneth Boulding (whose *Disarmament and the Economy* is quoted), Vance Bourjaily, and—anticlimax of anticlimaxes—Leonard Lewin. All roads, however, lead to Leonard Lewin: he is a freelance journalist who has reviewed a book on think-tanks, he edited *A Treasury of Political Humor,* and he loaned a working draft of the *Report* to a *Trans-action* informant.

The *Report* is far from being "just a hoax," though,

and it cannot be dismissed out of hand. Despite its many specious arguments and its spotty knowledge of social science, it is also an acutely accurate satire. What it satirizes is explained by John Doe: ". . . what they wanted from us was a different kind of *thinking*. It was a matter of approach. Herman Kahn calls it 'Byzantine' —no agonizing over cultural and religious values. It is the kind of thinking that Rand and the Hudson Institute and [the Institute for Defense Analysis] brought into *war* planning. . . ." War-gaming has become peace-gaming.

The fact is that the *Report* could have been compiled entirely from authentic sources. There are many social scientists doing this kind of investigation; there are members of the Defense Department who think like this. As one reader has observed, "This provides a better rationale of the U.S. Government's posture today than the Government's official spokesmen have provided. A better title for the book, in fact, would have been the same as Norman Mailer's novel: *Why Are We in Vietnam?*"

The threat that the *Report* holds is not so much that it will be believed and acted upon, but that it *has* been believed and acted upon. Significantly, *Trans-action* has found that those readers who take the book seriously tend to be Government officials. Upon inquiry, sources very close to the White House were authorized to say that the files and libraries of the Executive Office of the President have been reviewed, and although some reports in the general subject area covered by the *Report* were found, there was no record of this particular report. These sources believed, therefore, that no comment was appropriate at this time. Informally, they observed that their statement does not rule out the possibility that the *Report* was sponsored either in the White House, by some Congressional committee, or by some other agency within the Federal Establishment.

More important than the need to know whether *Report from Iron Mountain* is authentic or not, the public needs to know what the current thinking of U.S. Government agencies is in regard to (1) what problems the United States would face in the event of peace and disarmament and (2) what programs should be devised to deal with these problems.

One Defense Department informant has admitted that some of his colleagues have agreed with the *Report*'s conclusion that the Vietnam war is sound because at least it helps preserve stability at home. Another informant, who works at the highest levels in strategic planning within the Pentagon, asserted after reading the *Report* that he saw no reason to consider it a hoax, since he often comes upon reports that read in much the same way. Yet a third person—a recent alumnus of the defense Establishment—found the *Report* quite credible. All this testifies to the enormous gap between secret Governmental assessments of questions of war and peace, of disarmament, and of the "war system" and official public stances—as much as it testifies to Mr. Lewin's skill as a creator of social-science fiction.

The publication of *Report from Iron Mountain,* whatever its source, should become an occasion for a new public demand for a penetrating examination and evaluation of Government reports on strategic planning for disarmament and peace. The extent to which a belief in the desirability and inevitability of "the war system" is built into the operational conceptions of the Government is of deepest public concern, not to be thwarted by claims that these are matters of state that require secrecy.

—*Irving L. Horowitz*

HENRY S. ROWEN

The most interesting aspect of the *Report* is the reaction to it in the press and among reviewers. It has been described as "original," "acute," "skillful," "chilling," "genuine." It is none of these. It is superficial and lacking in bite. That it should create a certain commotion is, perhaps, more a reflection on the generally low level of public discussion on matters of strategy, international affairs, and disarmament than anything else.

The consequences of disarmament or, to use the terminology of the *Report,* the abandonment of the "war-system" is certainly a subject worthy of serious discussion. So it is conceivably worthy of satire. After all, the U.S. Government supports the objective of general and complete disarmament. If that state of affairs, however it might be defined, were to be brought about, it would certainly be associated with a profound change in relations among states and even within them. And given the variety of opinions to be found in our society, there may be some people who hold a position resembling that presented in the *Report.* Evidently some reviewers think so. But for most of the arguments put forward in the *Report,* I can find little substance in fact, nor can I identify the advocates of the view held.

Statements such as "An economy as advanced and complex as our own requires the planned average annual destruction of not less than 10 percent of gross national product . . . ," or "As an economic substitute for war [a social program] is inadequate because it would be far too cheap," or "the rate of pollution could be increased . . ." in order to have an enemy to fight, or the suggestion that slavery be reintroduced to our society in order to maintain social control, are not ludicrous versions of serious views; they are merely ludicrous.

Most of the *Report* deals with the social and economic effects within the nation state of general and complete disarmament. The *Report* has little to say about the international consequences of disarmament. Here it has largely overlooked what those who "commissioned" the *Report* might have expected as an essential topic for discussion. It is characteristic of the casual nature of this work that it fails to cite Tom Schelling's original and important observations on the consequences of "total" disarmament and to deal with the issues he raises. (Thomas C. Schelling, "The Role of Deterrence in Total Disarmament," *Foreign Affairs,* April 1962.)

Finally, the *Report* would have a greater effect if it had more of the marks of a genuine, Establishment-commissioned product. The little things—concessions, references to contemporary international affairs, hedges, touching of the bureaucratic bases—are largely missing.

MARC PILISUK

There are several cogent issues raised by *Report from Iron Mountain.* Among them, the question of whether or not the enterprise is a satirical hoax (and I tend to favor this view) seems to matter least.

The fact is that the enterprise is distinctly reminiscent of the style, procedures, and tone of the new operations-oriented, free-wheeling brainstormers whose product is sold and solicited in policy circles as serious social-science analysis. In fact, the *Report* recalls these brainstormers with sufficient vividness to make us quake with fear about the process that does go on.

The early sections deal with the composition of the Special Study Group, and its indoctrination to answer the question set forth without bias. The method previews one that may soon be improved upon, as follows: Add 250 hours of behavioral-scientist time to seven full-time hardware types, one ex-intelligence man, one international-relations type with government experience, two successful industrialists, a regional planner, an eminent physicist, and a Negro (even if the last, because of the demand, must be rented from Hertz). To promote frankness, lubricate the group with some unspeakable jokes or rudeness. In the first section of the final report, insist that one has cornered the market on objectivity and has been able to transgress, in all subsequent conclusions, the moral sensibilities that hinder other mortals. The technique will eventually be amended to include abbreviated T-group (sensitivity-training) sessions, and will then claim that the participants will thereby have achieved either the equivalent of a psychoanalysis or, at least, the Dhyana of the ancient Buddhists. This emphasis upon gaining a virtual monopoly on truth by the purity of the group's cathartic expurgation, or by its own surprise when it saw the light, is something that distinguishes the possessed individual or group from the skeptical scientist or philosopher. The latter, however forceful about their current beliefs, remain dubious about the ultimate validity of these beliefs.

Because the technique is simple and because it disdains the hard work of the social scientist is not sufficient reason to reject the *Report*'s conclusions. With reference to finding an alternative to war, most serious social-science research, as the *Report* suggests, has been trivial—if not in its relevance or in the validity of its conclusions, at least in the paucity of its attempts to find an adequate answer to the question of why its research is not being put to use. Moreover, since empirical research requires some operational statement of what one is talking about, and studies come easier where the topic is limited in scope, few social scientists ever devote themselves to prolonged analysis of how or why the social system *as a whole* evolves into war or peace. Some serious scholars have written about the economics of disarmament (usually with the conclusion that it is manageable, given a pattern of resource reallocations and planning that is about as impossible as disarmament itself). Psychiatrists, anthropologists, and ethologists have written about aggression and violent war (usually with the conclusion that in man, at least, bloodless forms of hostile behavior and of resolving disputes may be possible). Other social scientists have produced a host of ingenious solutions—international armies, agencies, exchanges, alliances, friendships, detection techniques, and so on—all of which have been explored separately. But it is rare to find anyone brash enough to take on the whole gamut of questions at once. In this, *Report from Iron Mountain* stands out. It covers a broad expanse; refers with some familiarity to relevant literature in several fields; and creates hypothetical projections with the gusto of a first-year student in urban architecture creating a city.

The *Report* contributes some penetrating insights into the system of the think-tank operation. One is the use of consensual validation among like-minded people to replace evidence. "It was hard to figure out who were the liberals and who were the conservatives, or who were hawks and who were doves." Shown here are the limits of American pluralism as a check on military-industrial power. Real power determines not who wins out among various political protagonists, but who decides the smorgasbord of which protagonists or which issues will be considered. A currently circulating definition of a dove is: One who favors the least escalation. If pluralism is to operate, it requires something more than this as a counterpower to military interests.

A second insight into the think tank is the use of computer programs to resolve problems for which gross assumptions must be made (and then forgotten) so that the product can have a ring of scientific jargon that sounds good, or at least incomprehensibly authoritative, when presented in Congressional testimony or in special White House reports. Here the gem is the "peace games" method, described as a computer language with a superior capacity to interrelate data with no apparent common points of reference. The product of this method is illustrated with great poignancy in a footnote that explains the prediction that science could still continue to progress for two more decades after the end of the war system:

"This rather optimistic estimate was derived by plotting a three-dimensional distribution of three arbitrarily defined variables: the macro-structural, re-lating to the extension of knowledge beyond the capacity of conscious experience; the organic, dealing with the manifestations of terrestrial life as inherently comprehensible; and the infra-particular, covering the conceptual requirements of natural phenomena. Values were assigned to the known and unknown in each parameter, tested against data from earlier chronologies, and modified heuristically until predictable correlations reached a useful level of accuracy. 'Two decades' means, in this case, 20.6 years, with a standard deviation of only 1.8 years. (An incidental finding, not pursued to the same degree of accuracy, suggests a greatly accelerated resolution of issues in the biological sciences after 1972.)''

A third characteristic of the think-tank approach is a willingness to promote the causes of some morally-handicapped diviner of the future of mankind. The strategic framework, unhampered by sentiment, assumes that Machiavellian motivation and violence are not only real, but necessary for the best interests of society. If they lead to a destruction of most of society, so be it: The realist faces this prospect and looks beyond. Just as Herman Kahn can deduce the promising opportunities available in the post-nuclear-attack era, so does *Report from Iron Mountain* speak about the population-control advantages of nuclear weapons. Formerly, wars hurt the species by selectively killing off the strongest of its members. The species is now, fortunately, in for a better deal, according to the *Report*, since nuclear weapons will kill indiscriminately. Of course, the *Report* indicates that this gain in the gene pool may be offset by some genetic damage to the survivors (just as Herman Kahn notes, in *On Escalation*, that a nuclear exchange may produce casualties). But at least the stability of our social system would not be jeopardized by disarmament, withdrawal, idealism, or refusal to play the strategic game.

Behind all this satire, the book contains a provocative analysis of how dependent this country is upon war for the centralized planning and domination of resources and personnel that keep the society from embarking upon radical departures from its traditions. That this central argument is shored up by some apparently unfounded assumptions regarding the significance of killing to the culture, arts, science, and even the existence of social systems does not make the argument less valid. Two years ago I did some research into the military-industrial complex and came to an essentially similar conclusion, namely that American society, as we now know it, could *not* make the accommodations necessary to achieve disarmament reallocations, to achieve assistance of the type needed to avert extensive violence stemming from underdevelopment, or to achieve international jurisdiction of disputes.

If the conclusion that current American society is incompatible with peace is valid, the recommendations one makes still depend upon values. *Report from Iron Mountain* remains true to its asserted heritage of the assumed source of all great values, the war system, and it concludes that peace is not to be obtained or desired. Perhaps the recommendation is prophetic for, beneath the rationalizations and moralisms, American policy does continue to make the choices that make future violent conflict inevitable. Still, there are those among us who follow Jeffersonian values and would recommend instead that it is the American system, rather than peace, that has grown dangerous and unresponsive to our needs. Perhaps the United States, rather than peace, is the appropriate target for revolutionary restructuring. The *Report* is one attempt to hasten this process through exposure.

There is danger as well as promise in such satire. During the fallout-shelter controversy, a brilliant piece appeared in *New University Thought* entitled "On Serving Your Fellow Man." It dealt with the problems of convincing people of the advantages of (and overcoming their aversions to) orderly cannibalism in the food-depleted shelter. The approach ranged from the problem of ethics (serving the greatest number with the fewest number) to the problems of appetite (better recipes and prestige-advertising inducements). It was, unfortunately, no more absurd in its rationale than any other part of the shelter program. But I shuddered at the time to think that some secret Special Study Group —imbued with dedication and freed from emotional or moral compunctions—might pick up the suggestion and immediately engage in the technical problem of how to promote this new dimension in shelter living.

We have come a long way when the existing think tanks can plan for levels of genocide matter of factly and with only an occasional need even for secrecy. The *Report* stirs revulsion only in those who play the game in which people count. For the strategy theorists, and that may by now include too many of us, I fear that they have just picked up a trick or two that they might otherwise have missed.

I have been asked twice now whether I wrote the book. I did not. Anatol Rapoport, Kenneth Boulding,

Noam Chomsky, Paul Goodman, Donald Michael, Amitai Etzioni, and Irving Horowitz are candidates whose wit, competence, and devotion to peace make them suspect. My great hope, however dim, is that it was done by some dropout from the RAND Corporation as an overture to his reentry into the family of man. My great fear is that the strategic framework of thought is so prevalent and so compatible with the competitive advantage of an affluent society that the *Report* describes a process of controlling the future that is too far along for warnings to be of value.

MURRAY WEIDENBAUM

From the newspaper articles alone, I could not figure out why Mr. Lewin modestly wished to cloak his work in semi-anonymity. A reading of the volume clears up that question rapidly. If this string of unsupported assertions and social-science fiction had been offered under his own name, it would have been laughed off the market as the malevolent musings of an uninformed crackpot.

I particularly regret seeing the numerous factual and analytical errors included in the sections dealing with economics. The general reader is likely to be hard put to separate fact from fiction. For example, "The Special Study Group" repeats the tiresome Marxian cliché that the Vietnam war was stepped up in 1965 "in the usual coordination . . . with dangerously rising unemployment rates." How should the general reader be expected to know that the truth of the matter was just the opposite? Unemployment rates—and total unemployment—were falling all through 1965 *prior* to the

Vietnam buildup during the middle of the year. The unemployment rate was 5.2 percent in 1964. It declined from 5.0 percent in February 1965 to 4.5 percent in July 1965. It is hard to believe that such basic distortion of the truth is not malevolent.

Perhaps a more fundamental flaw is the author's contention that the economic and fiscal tools of Federal budget policy would not be effective enough to facilitate the shift of resources from military to civilian uses. The discussion here (page 21) is particularly illogical. First the reader is told that fiscal tools "can provide new incentives in the economy." In the very next sentence, the author states that these tools "reflect the economy; they do not motivate it." (My colleagues in sociology tell me that the sociological sections of *Iron Mountain* are poor, but that the economics chapter seems to be convincing. I will leave to the psychologists the analysis of how to con academics via "interdisciplinary" research.)

Any student of Economics 1 knows that government purchases of goods and services are indeed a source of "final" demand, that the Federal Government's buying of tables or chairs or post-office buildings or space satellites motivates private production and employment just as directly as private customers do. Witness the substantial shift of resources from civilian output to meet the needs of the Vietnam war.

Incidentally, this large and rapid shift of resources also belies the alleged geographical "inflexibility" of military production. The step-up in the Vietnam war has resulted in major shifts in the geographic, industrial, and occupational distribution of military purchasing in the American economy. While some Midwestern states have seen their military contracts double during the last few years, during the same period several of the far Western states—Washington, Utah, and Colorado—have had their defense orders virtually cut in half.

The industrial shifts in military demand during the last few years have been equally dramatic and belie the author's statement that "rigid specialization . . . characterizes modern war production." While the large aerospace and electronics firms have been obtaining declining shares of the military market, clothing and textile orders are up 240 percent, automotive vehicles are up 80 percent, and food is up 60 percent. Details are contained in *Economy Effect of Vietnam Spending,* Joint Economic Committee (Washington, G.P.O., 1967, 2 vols.).

Perhaps the greatest disservice that *Iron Mountain* renders is to lower the level of argument in the crucial dialogue on the prospects for peace. Until now the debates have centered mainly on different interpretations of a common factual basis. We are now reduced to the lower-level chore of cleaning up Lewin's literary litter before it pollutes the intellectual environment. Under the circumstances, it is unfortunate that *Iron Mountain* is receiving greater academic attention than its spiritual ancestor, that earlier anonymous and allegedly suppressed committee report, the *Protocols of the Elders of Zion.*

LEONARD J. DUHL

Whether this book is a hoax or not is irrelevant. What is important is the fact that it exists, and that it reflects a particular style of thinking.

Report from Iron Mountain serves a useful function in pointing out that a peacetime society needs new kinds of social planning to deal with the special problems created by peace. But the book points out this need with that type of long-range thinking that treats ecological models—models that incorporate demographic and geographic variables as well as sociological ones—as completely closed, almost fully controllable, rigid systems.

Irving Louis Horowitz has suggested that fascists use ecology as a model because it gives them their excuse for massive control—for control not just of matters we usually consider the legitimate concerns of government, but of matters (such as who will have children and who will not) that democratic systems consider the business of their individual citizens. An ecological model need not serve such fascistic ends, however. Treated as an open system, an ecological model for social planning can actually help ensure the survival of democratic procedures during the critical adjustments that our society will have to undergo, now and in the future, in order to adapt itself to a state of peace.

The essential fault of the *Report* is its failure to recognize (1) that planning from an ecological model, whether for war or peace, is a *process*—rather than the establishment of a set of rigid systems, and (2) that this process is not oriented toward stability, but toward change.

Our economic, sociological, ecological, cultural, and scientific concerns are concerns for those processes that permit change to occur in each system. The overall social system we seek to preserve is not what the *Report* calls "the survival of the social system we know today." Nor is it based solely upon a set of institutions for which "substitute" institutions must be created. Rather, it is a fluid system composed of changing institutions and processes through which we seek to enable every individual to control and affect the events that control his life.

If one views the problem of peace as an issue we must face, as the *Report* does, one must then give high priority to domestic concerns. And these concerns extend beyond the static and negative one defined by the *Report* as "the survival of social systems we know today." They are, instead, the development of new social systems—and modifications of existing ones—to permit the kind of domestic processes that will enable us to solve our internal problems without turning into a fascistic, controlled, or militaristic state. They require changes toward improvement, rather than merely viewing the stability of society as the "one bedrock value that cannot be avoided."

Certainly the two poles may be anarchy and control. But the planning procedures needed to ensure that our peacetime social system is between these two poles are not those that maximize the value of stability, but those concerned with creating mechanisms to guarantee that the values we hold dear to our society are maintained. How to create these mechanisms so that we can further human development, achieve health, and maximize citizen participation in those events that affect our lives—these are the important questions to which all else must be directed. And these are the questions that the *Report* fails to ask.

A peacetime society in which these mechanisms exist may not be perfectly stable and free of tensions. But social tensions are not war. Society can prepare itself for the tensions accompanying the negotiations for change that permit a society to be viable and active.

That social scientists would permit themselves to become party to a fascistic goal, as they have if this *Report* is real, truly requires that they reexamine their goals for our society. Years ago Kurt Lewin, in *Resolving Social Conflicts* (Harper & Row, 1948), said:

"it seems to be crucial for the problems of social science that the practitioner understand that through social science and only through it can he hope to gain the power necessary to do a good job. Unfortunately, there is nothing in social law and social research which will force the practitioner towards good. Science gives more freedom and power to both the doctor and the murderer, to democracy and Fascism. The social scientist should recognize his responsibility also in respect to this."

Report from Iron Mountain illustrates that the social scientist must reexamine any tendencies he has to define what is good as what is static and structured. It reveals how an ecological model can be twisted into a highly institutionalized and status-quo-oriented approach that negates the essence of ecology—change, and the participation of all segments of a system in the processes through which that change occurs.

January/February 1968

Children of the Laboratory

HELEN P. GOULDNER

An adopted child frequently suffers painful problems in identity. When he asks, "Who am I?" he often quite literally means "Where did I come from?" This question is difficult for adoptive parents to answer and their attempts, whether straightforward or evasive, often create difficulties for the child.

But these problems may be even more difficult in the future when the child who asks the questions is not adopted, but born as a result of revolutionary medical and biological developments—in artificial insemination, artificial inovulation, and the manipulation of genetic materials. The child whose biological mother or father is an anonymous donor, or whose life began as an embryo "in vitro," or whose mother submitted to major genetic surgery, will very likely ask the same question—"Who am I?" What hope is there that he will receive an answer he can live with?

Even the field of adoption itself—with its problems of legitimacy (most non-kin adoptions involve illegitimate children), inheritance, and created family relationships—will be affected by the medical and biological breakthroughs. Since most non-kin adoptions are by couples unable to conceive, the institution of adoption will probably give way as couples make use of increased biological knowledge and control. Most of the remaining non-kin adopters will be couples in which the woman is unable to bear a child because of some organic handicap. But even here there remains the biological possibility, now being seriously considered, of another woman, much like a wet nurse, carrying and giving birth to the handicapped woman's child.

Yet even as adoption itself wanes, the theories and ideas developed, debated, and still contested in adoption will eventually provide precedents, if not the central model, for answers to the problems raised by the new biology. I say *eventually,* because it does not appear that the people shaping the decisions in artificial insemination, the harbinger of the biological revolution, are presently taking account of the psychological and sociological knowledge concerning adoption.

One important reason, I believe, that adoption knowledge is not yet shaping practices in artifical insemination is the erroneous assumption that the child—the "produced" child—will never know the circumstances of his conception. Hence it is assumed that he is in a much different situation from that of the adopted child. The assumption that the child will not be told, or will not discover, that he has been "produced" is naive.

It seems highly likely that someone at some time will tell, for people enjoy secrets too much to keep them. He may be told by the parents—perhaps in guilty confession

—or in an angry outburst by a friend or relative. The discovery possibilities are endless. He may overhear a conversation, or in an attempt to piece together occasional strange looks and comments from his parents, he may come to the conclusion himself. It would be remarkable for a mother and father to live 20 years with a child without giving away the secret. And it is another question as to what the family would have to pay, in the strains of parent-child relations, if the secret is actually kept. It is true that parents keep important secrets from their children (or at least they try), and that children certainly keep important secrets from their parents. But keeping knowledge of the child's heritage from him will not only involve a long series of evasions, but quite likely some outright lies; for sooner or later almost all children ask, in one way or another, "Are you my real parents?"

It is assumed here, then, that while there are differences, the produced child and his family will have much in common with the adopted child and his family. The knowledge gained in adoption practices may thus provide some guidelines. Of course, not all the answers have been found in adoption—far from it. There are a number of problems that have never been solved and probably cannot be solved within the basic framework of the institution of adoption. But however unsatisfactory adoption has been as a model, it may still teach us much about the social arrangements needed to accompany the new biological revolution. At the very least, the unsolved problems—the recurrent social-psychological difficulties of adopted children—will forewarn us about the problems of the produced child.

My own research and that of others indicates that, especially as he reaches adolescence, the adopted child faces strain in coping with the "stigma" of being adopted and with special problems in resolving his identity. There is every reason to assume that at least the first few generations of produced children will face a similar situation.

There are many types of people who are looked upon as being "different" while at the same time more or less accepted by those around them. The disfigured, the crippled, the blind, the unusually tall or exceptionally short, are among such types. Erving Goffman has described their difficulties: Because the individual is defined as being somehow different (but may not define himself as different) there is not only strain in everyday relationships with "normals," but much inward confusion and possible self-deprecation.

Both the adopted and the produced are "different" from "normals," and they are different in a crucial way. Most societies we know about have strong feelings about biological heritage—not so much in terms of whether a particular heritage is "good" or "bad" but simply in *knowing* it. (We can joke about the skeleton in the closet; we do not joke about an unknown mother or father.) Although the evidence is fragmentary, it suggests that because of their frequently unknown heritage (even with increasingly liberal attitudes in our own society), adopted persons are regarded ambivalently by large segments of the population. There is no reason not to expect the same for the produced child.

Note, for example, the frequency with which the news media pointedly refer to the fact that a celebrity's child is adopted, be it by the late General MacArthur, Elizabeth Taylor, or Sammy Davis, Jr. There is also a proliferation of problem-oriented literature on some variation of the theme of how to raise an adopted child. The very quantity of such books and articles both here and in Western Europe certainly implies that the adopted child may present special problems, as does the exceptional or handicapped child.

(Their quantity also suggests that even if the adopted child has no problems, his parents do.) And just as parents of other "different" children often form groups to discuss various common problems so, too, groups of adoptive parents are commonplace.

By reviewing some research on adopted children, we may be able to draw some implications concerning the prospective problems of produced children.

H. David Kirk's research on adoption, summarized in his book, *Shared Fate,* includes studies of community reactions to a family's discussion or announcement of the adoption of a baby. These frequently include a patronizing compliment ("What a wonderful thing for you to do!") or rejection ("How do you know what you are going to get?" or "Blood will tell.").

One questionnaire a student of mine gave to a class of 54 women at a small Midwest college indicated that more than half were uneasy about speaking of ancestry or heritage around someone they knew was adopted; more than a third felt "sorry" for an adopted child; and almost all wondered how adopted people felt about being adopted.

How do the adopted themselves perceive the attitudes of those around them? Many feel, to some degree, stigmatized. The young adopted people we studied (and the popular literature) report childhood incidents of being taunted by other children, of overhearing family arguments about inheritance rights, family resemblances, or the wisdom of adoption, and of grudging acceptance and sometimes outright rejection by some relatives. One girl reports, for example, that her parents had completely broken off relationships with her mother's family because once, at a large family gathering, the grandmother said for all to hear: "How could you be so irresponsible as to adopt two such horrible children?"

Adopted young people also frequently perceive some ambivalence in their parents. This ambivalence takes several forms. Our respondents tell of incidents where the parents, in an outburst of anger or irritation with them, would in some way blame the adoption: "I should never have gone to the trouble of getting you!" or "It must be your blood." There were not many such memories reported, but when they did occur they were remembered vividly. Several described, too, the thinly veiled anxiety of their parents when they began to date—anxiety that they, too, might have children out of wedlock. As one girl put it, "I know my mother is worried I'll turn out like my real mother." And another, "Sometimes my parents talk about being adopted in ways that aren't fair. When I go out on a date, they always seem to find some reason to bring it up." Another form of ambivalence is expressed in the feeling of adoptees that many of their normal growing pains are continually related to their being adopted. They feel both rejection and resentment: "Why can't I be just like anyone else and make the same mistakes as anyone else?"

To what extent this felt ambivalence is a projection of the adopted's own anxieties we cannot tell. However, the available data indicate that many adoptive parents continue to experience unsolved difficulties concerning their inability to procreate. If intense, these would certainly be reflected in some ambivalence toward the adopted child. (This is *not* to say, however, that the data indicate lack of love and affection in the adoptive family; on the contrary, there is no evidence that the adopted child is any better or any worse off than any other child in this respect.)

One result of the parental ambivalence is a reluctance of young people to discuss adoption with their parents when in adolescence the problem becomes of some concern.

The young people we studied often said things like, "I don't talk about it much for fear it would hurt them," and several expressed the feeling that it would be embarrassing. One adoptee reported that she had never really discussed her adoption with her parents:

In my sophomore year I decided to write a paper on adoption and to include some personal history. I called up my parents to ask them about it. They told me there was a safety deposit box down at the bank with all the things concerning my adoption in it. After talking to them, I felt like I had sort of hurt them. They sounded as if they thought I was dissatisfied. The next night I called them back up and told them I didn't really want to know although they told me I was old enough to know. I'm curious, but I don't really want to know. I've always thought of them as my parents. Parents mean more than just giving you life.

Adopted persons may hesitate to tell others they are adopted, for when it is revealed there is usually some difficulty in managing the situation. Friends, to quote from our respondents, are often "dumbfounded" and either react with an embarrassed silence or with some inanity: "Oh, really, isn't that nice," or "I *never* would have guessed." Again, as one said with some disgust, "They always ask stupid questions like 'What does it feel like to be adopted?'" Once revealed, the adoption may create further difficulties in subsequent conversations about nationality, heritage, marriage, and children. One adopted person indicated that she rarely told anyone she was adopted "not only because of the prejudice, but because if I ever do anything bad they simply will say it's bad blood."

As might be expected, the adopted often develop a "line" or repertoire of ready-made answers to questions concerning adoption, some of which involve a kind of game-playing with the uninitiated. We asked the question, "What do you say when someone says you look like your parents?" Here are some responses:

—That's nice. And then I follow by saying, "I'm not theirs—I was adopted."

—I say "Impossible!" and then let the matter drop.

—Nothing. I'm not really embarrassed but I don't know what to say. I guess it is a type of embarrassment, kind of uneasy.

—Actually, it's never happened. If someone said I looked like my mother, I'd consider it a compliment and say, "Thank you." Later I'd tell Mother about it and we'd have a good roar.

Like all of us, the adopted are not above using their own special "difference" to gain attention. For example, after a long conversation about illegitimacy or heritage in a college bull session, the adopted person would announce to his stunned audience, "Well, you know I'm adopted." Or, as one adoptee said, "I like to shock people by telling them that someday I'm going to marry my brother."

The feeling of many adoptees that they are "different" is frequently expressed as a sense that they are somehow "unique" or "special"; some come pretty close to actually believing they *are* a "chosen one." (One of the most popular books on adoption for many years has been *The Chosen Baby*.) In fact, most of the young people we studied remembered having been told, in one form or another, that they had been "chosen." For example, in response to the question, "How did your parents tell you you were adopted," there were such answers as:

—All I can remember is that they said they picked me up, really wanted me, picked me out of several other babies.

—When they were joking they said they found me under a cabbage leaf. When they were serious they said they wanted a child and couldn't have one and hunted until they found me.

—My mother said when she put me to bed that I was her special little adopted girl and that she chose me.

—They told me God decided who was to have children and they couldn't. God willed I was born and they adopted me.

—They used to tell me they didn't have to take what came—that they chose me.

One of the favorite remembered retorts to other children who commented on their being adopted was, "I was chosen, your parents had no choice."

A related theme that ran through almost all of our interviews was an expression of overwhelming gratitude, sometimes bordering on guilt, toward the adoptive parents:

—I owe them so much—more than they owe me.

—They didn't have to raise me but they did and it was a favor to me. I often think of what I might have been if I had not been adopted.

—I *have* to be a success since they have done so much for me.

—They wanted us enough to go through all that red tape.

—I would never do anything to hurt them.

—I had diabetes when I was three years old, and my parents accepted it anyway.

This gratitude toward the parents, which sometimes makes it difficult for the young person to break away from the parental home, as well as the feelings of being "special," are related, I believe, to a set of child-rearing patterns in which adoption has been overly stressed—although many times unwittingly. Kirk's data report intense attempts of the adoptive family to make the child feel loved and integrated into the family unit. He points out that these attempts, when the child is young, may later make it difficult for the child to become autonomous; family integration may be stressed at the expense of the independence of family members.

While the available data do not allow us to estimate just how stigmatizing adoption is, and we can only speculate on the forms that it takes, we do know that adopted persons feel different, and sometimes uncomfortably so. In Goffman's words:

> The special situation of the stigmatized is that society tells him he is a member of the wider group, which means he is a normal human being, but that he is also "different" in some degree, and that it would be foolish to deny this difference.

Some of the placement practices still used by many agencies—such as "matching" the child with adoptive parents or giving limited knowledge of the biological ancestry of the child to the family—encourage a denial of this difference. Kirk recognized this as one type of child-rearing pattern in which every attempt is made to minimize the adoptive status of the child. Such a pattern would involve, among other things, a reluctance to discuss the child's origins with him. In contrast, what Kirk saw as another pattern, that of "acknowledgement of difference," would involve, among other things, open acceptance and full discussion of his biological heritage and the circumstances of his birth. Practices involving this latter conception appear to be gaining vogue among adoption workers, both in the United States and Western Europe.

We have as yet no systematic comparison of the outcome of adoption in families in which one or the other pattern predominates. My impression from the fragmentary literature and from our own data is that where adoption is fully acknowledged, accepted, and openly discussed—while (and this is important) not overemphasized—young people who were adopted in infancy have less anxiety about their adoptive status and can cope with their "difference" without feeling particularly unique. However, a great deal of stress on the adoptive status (particularly an overemphasis on the fairy tale stories about "being especially chosen") may not only tie the young person too closely to his family, but also give him a feeling of hollow superiority that stands in the way of his coming to terms with his real difference.

It has been *au courant* to explain the various stresses and strains of late adolescence and early adulthood under the umbrella of "identity crises." There often occurs a sense of fragmented self, expressed by such sad but cliché phrases as, "I don't know who I am" or "Everything seems so meaningless and worthless."

While there is little research that specifically studies identity problems in adopted young people, what data there are suggest that they occur with considerable intensity. This is not surprising considering the ambivalent attitudes of middle class Americans toward illegitimacy, the limited information given to the adopting parents about the child's biological parents (particularly the biological father), the anxiety with which many adoptive parents communicate even the little known about the biological parents, and the continued emphasis on the importance of blood lines with some stigma correspondingly attached to being adopted. As Nathan M. Simon and Audrey G. Senturia put it in their paper "Adoption and Psychiatric Illness," the adopted young person's "fantasies about who he is are believed to be more intense because they are grounded in reality." In some important sense, to know our past is, in part, to know *who* we are.

Data from psychiatric studies of adopted young people reflect these identity problems. There is some evidence that the adopted experience a somewhat higher frequency of psychiatric problems than the non-adopted, particularly in childhood and adolescence. More precisely, the incidence of adopted children who seek aid in psychiatric facilities is proportionately slightly higher than the non-adopted. To what degree these data reflect the sensitivity of adoptive parents—their "agency proneness"—to the problems of their children has not been conclusively determined. It may indeed be true that adopted persons are not more prone to emotional illness, but that their adoptive parents are more prone to seek consultation. The psychiatric data do indicate, however, that where such illnesses occur there is a very strong likelihood that the illness will be exacerbated by the adoptive status.

The psychiatric problems of adopted children and adolescents lie most frequently in areas of sexual and aggressive behavior. According to several reports, their problems may stem from the inability to reconcile their images of the "good" adoptive parents and the "bad" biological parents. Conversely, some of our own respondents admitted that when they were having difficulty with their adoptive parents they often had fantasies about finding their "good" biological parents who might take them away from their "bad" adoptive parents!

Whether we wish to call it a problem of identity or not, our data clearly illustrate the extra load, under the best of circumstances, that the adopted must bear through adolescence and young adulthood. If he knows nothing of his biological heritage he weaves elaborate fantasies about it—frequently with guilt because he does not want to hurt his parents. The question of a search for the natural parents comes up, although it is usually dismissed; he wonders how his girl friend will respond to the knowledge he is adopted; he is curious about what his own children will be like; and he struggles once again with his illegitimacy. As one adopted said, "Did you ever realize what an ugly word 'bastard' is?"

It is my impression, again, that the intensity of these struggles varies most directly with the amount of knowledge the child has of his biological heritage. It is, of course, also related to his parents' attitudes—how comfortable they are in discussing his heritage, their acceptance of his illegitimacy, and their recognition that adoption may be a difficult situation for the young person to manage. Adoptive parents are as prone to being hurt by their children as any other parents; the adopted young people we talked with implied that parents were especially susceptible when curiosity about heritage was interpreted as rejection.

Among other things, it would seem, then, that the more the parents and child know about the child's biological background the better. Agencies increasingly give as much information as they have of the biological parents and their families: names, national heritage, physical features, education, socio-economic background, interests, history of diseases, and so on. Indeed, a relatively common practice in the so-called independent (non-agency) adoptions is to arrange for a meeting of the natural mother and the adoptive parents. Yet here, of course, is the paradox in adoption. For such knowledge may aid the young person to seek and find his biological parents some day, with possible trauma to himself, to the biological parents, and to the adoptive parents. Is this better or worse than having no known biological heritage?

We have no way of knowing the degree to which produced children will be stigmatized, what kind of special child-rearing patterns their parents will use, or what kinds of attitudes the children will eventually have about their fate. But having studied adoption, we can make guesses.

The situation will be somewhat different, of course. For one thing, the child will probably not live in a general public of neighbors and relatives who know the circumstances of his conception as do adopted children. Whereas some parents still say to associates, "This is my adopted child," it is unlikely that in the near future they will say, "This is my artificially conceived child." Although it will be most difficult to keep the "secret" from the child, this does not mean it will be printed on the birth announcements or that his "conception birthday" will be celebrated regularly as many adoptive families celebrate the adoption date. However, there may come a day when it is socially acceptable to discuss such genetic origins openly so the child will see no discrepancy between his parents' attempts to inform him of his origin but to hide it from others.

For another thing, the stigma of adoption comes from its link with illegitimacy, the unknown, and rejection, all of which are lessened in biological manipulation. Great (if sometimes specious) effort is being made in artificial insemination cases to reduce the problem of illegitimacy, to make it "possible" that the husband is the biological father. *Newsweek* (November 15, 1965) reports:

To get around the question of legitimacy, doctors often advise AI [artificial insemination] couples to have intercourse shortly after the artificial insemination. "Since infertile men usually have at least some sperm," explains Fish [Dr. Stewart A. Fish, University of Arkansas], "no one can ever prove that the husband isn't the child's real father." Occasionally, husbands have cited AI in divorce proceedings to avoid paying child-support judgments. For this reason, some doctors make sure the AI donor and husband have the same blood types; thus making it difficult for the husband to prove he isn't the child's father.

In artificial insemination the mother is known. Further, the produced child will not have to cope with the inevitable question of the adopted child: "Why didn't they want me? Why did they give me away?"

Thus the situation will be different in some important respects, but there are still many similarities, so the produced child and his family will have to cope with some of the same problems as the adopted child and his family. For one thing, there are the questions of *whether* the child should be told, and *what* he should be told. The answer to the first, I believe, is the same as the answer from adoption workers (with some demurrers from psychiatrists):

He should be told, and should be told early, because he is going to find out anyway, and it is better to hear it from parents than from others.

As to what to tell him, the adoption data strongly indicate that he be given not fairy tale information (including being "specially chosen") but the straight story in a language he can understand. The data also suggests that he could use some information about his biological heritage. This means that the parents must have some information to give. An anonymous sperm bank may protect parents and donors, but what will it do in the long run to the child?

The produced child is also going to have to learn to live with his difference. Again, it appears that practices which encourage either overemphasis or denial of difference are unwise. Practices involving denial of difference may be obvious, such as withholding information about the child's conception. Or they may be more subtle: the so-called matching as to race, nationality, height, weight, IQ, hair and eye color; calling frequent attention to family resemblances; assigning the child the parent's national heritage even though it may not be the same. What data there are on adoption suggest that in the long run the best chances for the produced child, and possibly his parents, lie in recognizing the difference and in accepting the fact that it cannot be legalized, prayed, or wished away.

One of the advantages to a family that acknowledges that their child is different is that it helps the parents to accept *their* difference. This is still another similarity to the adoptive family, but one that may give more trouble. In most non-kin adoptions either the husband or wife is sterile; but they share a common enterprise in taking a child with a different heritage from either of theirs, whatever their subsequent difficulties about their inability to procreate may be. In artificial insemination, on the other hand, the mother bears the child from an unknown donor; the father is left with the knowledge that there is only the remotest of possibilities that the offspring is his biological child. The issue about whether or not the father must support the child in the case of divorce has already been raised in the courts. The very fact that such cases are pending opens serious questions about the day-to-day dynamics of family life. In the case of adoption Kirk suggests that if a child lives in a situation in which the parents accept *their* difference, the child will more readily accept *his*. This is why he calls his book *Shared Fate*.

Although there is now much secrecy concerning artificial insemination, news reports indicate that in the emerging practices the whole focus is clearly—and I believe wrongly—on a philosophy of denial of difference. To quote one typical report (*Newsweek,* November 15, 1965):

. . . AI [artificial insemination] is one of the best thera-peutic weapons we have. AI gives the prospective mother the emotional experience of pregnancy and delivery and is far less expensive than adoption. To make sure that AI babies are intellectually and physically normal, most physicians employ such persons as medical students or hospital residents as semen donors. . . . (Adopted babies, on the other hand, often may come from a less certain genetic background.) [sic.] Generally, donors are "matched" with husbands—physically, ethnically, and in hair and eye color. So that no one will know who the actual father is, a sample from a different donor may be used for each insemination.

As such news reports indicate, the main concern is for the doctors, the donors, and the parents. But what about the child?

April 1967

NOTES ON CONTRIBUTORS

Fred Davis   "Why All of Us May Be Hippies Some Day"

Professor of sociology at the University of California, San Francisco (San Francisco Medical Center). Davis is the author of *Passage Through Crisis, Polio Victims and Their Families*, and editor of *The Nursing Profession* and has written widely in the areas of social deviance and professional socialization.

Helen P. Gouldner   "Children of the Laboratory"

Professor of sociology at Washington University and coordinator of the undergraduate program there. Gouldner is author of *Analyzing Modern Organizations* and co-author of *Modern Sociology*.

Kenneth Keniston   "How Community Mental Health Helped Stamp Out the Riots"

Professor of psychiatry (psychology) at the Yale School of Medicine and director of the Behavioral Sciences Study Center there. Keniston is well known for his study of personality development in adolescence and early youth. His books include *The Uncommitted: Alienated Youth in American Society* and *Young Radicals: Notes on Committed Youth*.

Robert A. Skedgell   "How Computers Pick Election Winners"

With CBS radio and television since 1939 as writer, news editor, reporter, producer and administrator. In 1964 Skedgell was named director of vote profile analysis with CBS News. In 1967 he became CBS News Weekend News Manager.

Melvin M. Webber   "Politics of Information"

Professor of city planning at the University of California, Berkeley, where he is acting director of the Institute of Urban and Regional Development and chairman of the Center for Planning and Development Research. Webber has been editor of the *Journal of American Institute Planners* and consultant to numerous local and federal Agencies.